operation barbarossa 1941

army group south

ROBERT KIRCHUBEL

operation barbarossa 1941

army group south

Praeger Illustrated Military History Series

PRAEGER

Westport, Connecticut
London

Library of Congress Cataloging-in-Publication Data

Kirchubel, Robert.
Operation Barbarossa 1941: Army Group South / Robert Kirchubel.
p. cm – (Praeger illustrated military history, ISSN 1547-206X)
Originally published: Oxford: Osprey, 2003.
Includes bibliographical references and index.
ISBN 0-275-98282-3 (alk. paper)
1. World War, 1939–1945 – Campaigns – Eastern Front. 2. Germany. Heer. Armee
Heeresgruppe Sèd – History. 3. Soviet Union -- German occupation, 1941–1944. I.
Title. II. Series.
D764.K493 2004
940.54'217–dc22 2003063468

British Library Cataloguing in Publication Data is available.

First published in paperback in 2003 by Osprey Publishing Limited, Elms Court,
Chapel Way, Botley, Oxford OX2 9LP. All rights reserved.

Library of Congress Catalog Card Number: 2003063468
ISBN: 0-275-98282-3
ISSN: 1547-206X

Praeger Publishers, 88 Post Road West, Westport, CT 06881
An imprint of Greenwood Publishing Group, Inc.
www.praeger.com

Printed in China through World Print Ltd.

The paper used in this book complies with the Permanent Paper Standard issued
by the National Information Standards Organization (Z39.48-1984).

10 9 8 7 6 5 4 3 2 1

ILLUSTRATED BY: Howard Gerrard

CONTENTS

KEY TO MILITARY SYMBOLS

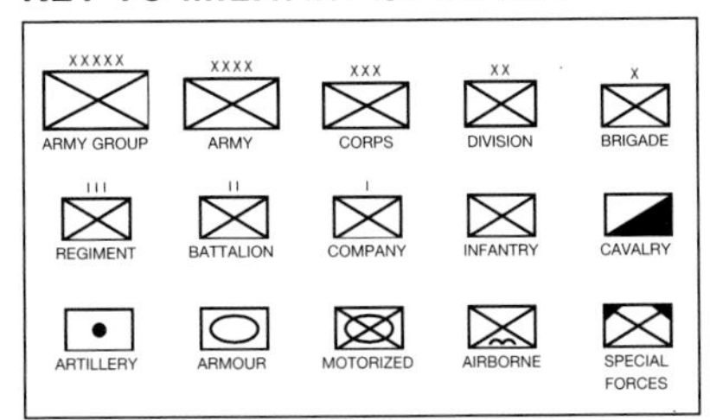

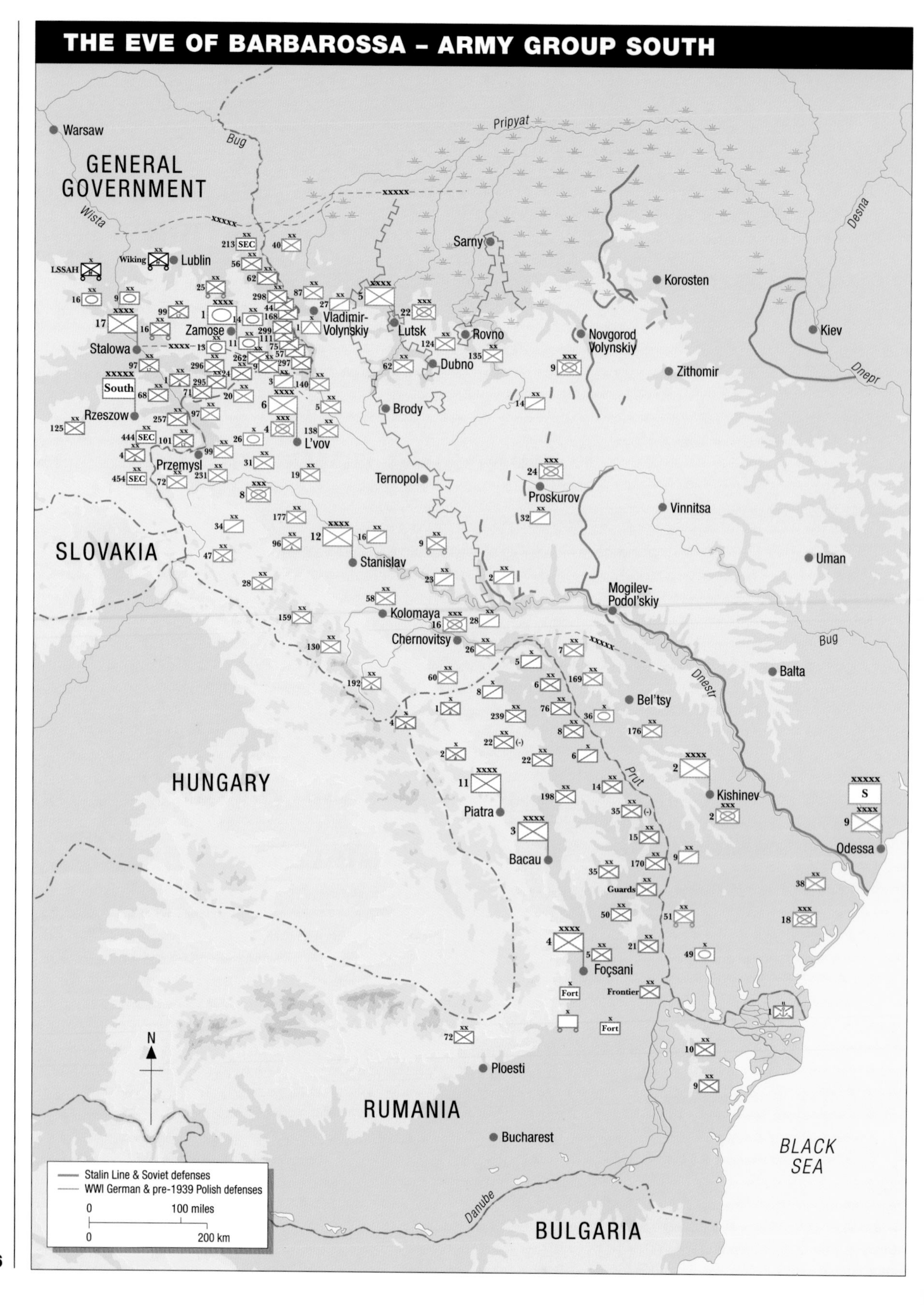
THE EVE OF BARBAROSSA – ARMY GROUP SOUTH
Warsaw
GENERAL GOVERNMENT
Bug
Pripyat
Wista
Lublin
Sarny
Korosten
Kiev
Desna
Vladimir-Volynskiy
Lutsk
Rovno
Novgorod Volynskiy
Zamose
Stalowa
Dubno
Zithomir
Dnepr
South
Rzeszow
Brody
L'vov
Przemysl
Ternopol
Proskurov
Vinnitsa
SLOVAKIA
Stanislav
Uman
Mogilev-Podol'skiy
Kolomaya
Chernovitsy
Bug
Dnestr
Balta
Bel'tsy
Prut
HUNGARY
Kishinev
Piatra
Bacau
Odessa
Foçsani
Ploesti
RUMANIA
Bucharest
BLACK SEA
BULGARIA
Danube
N
Stalin Line & Soviet defenses
WWI German & pre-1939 Polish defenses
0 100 miles
0 200 km

INTRODUCTION

Nazi Germany's invasion of the Soviet Union on 22 June 1941, Operation Barbarossa, has no equal in military history. By nearly any measure – numbers of combatants involved, physical scope, hatred and ruination – the Nazi–Soviet War was immense. The German Führer Adolf Hitler achieved strategic, operational and tactical surprise against an amply forewarned Josef Stalin. Rapacious Panzer Groups, supported overhead by the Luftwaffe, recorded daily advances of 30 and 40 miles. The bulk of the Wehrmacht marched on foot behind, closing off pockets of many hundreds of thousands of Red Army captives. Nazi Propaganda Minister Josef Goebbels demurred at showing the German people maps of the USSR while some Germans wondered if prior to launching Barbarossa Hitler had even seen such a map.

While the Soviet Union's immense landmass was obvious to anyone looking at a globe of the earth, the resilience of the Communist government, the toughness of the Red Army soldier and the ultimate wisdom of its leadership's conduct of the war came as an unexpected shock to the invaders and many observers. The Germans' initial opinion that they need only "kick in the door and the whole rotten structure will come crashing down" was not unreasonable given the collapse of the Tsarist and Provisional governments at the end of the Great War. From the very start the vicious border battles demonstrated to the Wehrmacht in the field, if not to its leaders behind, that Barbarossa would not be as easy as previous campaigns. Many Soviet soldiers, cut off behind the advancing enemy in huge encirclements did not give up but either fought to the death or joined civilian partisan bands. By the time

Hopeful prewar Soviet poster boasts "The borders of the USSR protect all the Soviet people." Even after the Wehrmacht had overrun most of Europe the Blitzkrieg's violence came as a shock to the USSR.

the first freezing weather hit in October the Wehrmacht was greatly weakened and still far from achieving most of its objectives.

Not just Hitler, but also his professional military staff, were almost unanimous in their rosy view of the invasion's projected results. Barbarossa's ultimate outcome was far from clear at any point during the summer of 1941. The Wehrmacht's "Blitzkrieg" – the combination of flexible mission-style orders, mechanization, airpower and communications – won victory after victory. Having vanquished the French, the world's "best army", the year before, Germany had unshakeable confidence in her armed forces, bordering on arrogance. The Soviet military did not exhibit signs of total collapse, however, nor did an alternative to the Communist system present itself. First Hitler then Stalin called for a total war of extermination and national survival. Interestingly, only in the two dictators' minds did the political and military strategy of either country coalesce. The war on the Eastern Front, and it might be argued Barbarossa itself, sealed the fate of Hitler's Third Reich and determined the outcome of World War II.

* * *

At 0100hrs on Sunday, 22 June 1941 Army Group South issued codeword "Wotan", indicating Barbarossa would begin as planned in little more than two hours. The German Army's senior officer, Field Marshal Gerd von Rundstedt, commanded 46½ divisions along a front of more than 800 miles. His headquarters, under Chief of Staff General of Infantry Georg von Sodenstern, had proved itself in France. Von Rundstedt managed the Reich's version of coalition warfare, with Hungarian, Italian, Rumanian and Slovakian formations under command. With the largest operational area of any Army Group, yet only one Panzer group, his men had four difficult tasks: Destroying Red Army units to their front; capturing the Ukrainian capital of Kiev and the Dnepr River crossings; seizing the Donets Basin (Donbas), and opening the route to the Caucasus oil region. Of the three army groups, von Rundstedt's came closest to accomplishing its assigned missions.

Facing Army Group South were the Kiev Special Military District and Odessa Military District, which at the start of the war became the Southwest and Southern Fronts respectively. Commanded by Lieutenant General M.P. Kirponos, the Southwest Front especially was well led, had some of the Red Army's best equipment and other benefits accrued from Stalin's belief that the south would be the Germans' main theater. Along the Black Sea coast Lieutenant General I.V. Tyulenev commanded the new Southern Front (originally the 9th Independent Army). Taking liberties with Stalin's orders not to make provocative gestures, both Military Districts had coordinated with NKVD Border troops and dispersed their aircraft. Soviet forces under their command offered a more skillful defense of the frontier than did the fronts facing Army Groups North and Center. Counterattacking as Red Army assets allowed and withdrawing to successive defense lines, they put von Rundstedt behind schedule.

Only when robbed of any operational freedom by Stalin's orders did true disaster hit Soviet defenders south of the Rokitno Marshes. Finally, in mid-September, and only with the cooperation of Army Group Center, von Rundstedt's forces achieved dramatic success. In the encirclement at Kiev, two-thirds of a million Soviet troops surrendered in history's greatest single military victory. For the first and only time in World War II German forces in the field outnumbered those of the USSR. Stalin's high command somehow plugged the resulting massive gap and resistance stiffened once again. Meanwhile, Hitler bled off mechanized forces from Army Group South for the attack on Moscow, German logistics foundered in the Ukrainian steppes, weather once more delayed von Rundstedt's advance and his troops reached the limit of their endurance. By November, the Donets River in the north, temporary possession of Rostov in the center and the siege lines around Sevastopol in the Crimea represented Army Group South's high water mark. Soon after the Soviets counterattacked along the entire front. By then, however, none of the senior commanders remained in their posts – Hitler had accepted von Rundstedt's resignation, Kirponos died at Kiev and Tyulenev went to the rear severely wounded.

ORIGINS OF THE CAMPAIGN

Hitler had two main reasons for launching Barbarossa: to carry out threats he had made since writing *Mein Kampf* and to remove any remaining British hope of continental assistance in the war. In the first case, a basic tenet of Nazism held that the vast lands to Germany's east were its for colonization and economic exploitation. Although Greater Germany was not overpopulated in 1941, Hitler sought *Lebensraum* (space to live) for the German people in the east. Similarly, Hitler thought Britain required "one demonstration of our military might" to acknowledge German dominance of the continent. On 9 January 1941 the Führer said, "After Russia's destruction Germany would be unassailable." Likewise, he made fuzzy linkages between the "Jewish-Anglo-Saxon warmongers" and the "Jewish rulers of Bolshevik-Muscovite Russia." Both factors combined to push Hitler toward a violent confrontation with the Soviet Union. The hitherto victorious Wehrmacht could translate his windy bombast into action.

Hitler saw the Molotov-Ribbentrop Treaty of 23 August 1939 as merely a disposable "tactical maneuver." Stalin was able, however, to control the flow of certain materials important to Germany's war effort. By the summer of 1940 a dangerous situation had developed: the USSR's industries required many of the same materials for the Red Army's rearmament program that Germany required. Hitler could not force Stalin to act as Germany's long-term supplier and it was against this background that Soviet Foreign Minister V.M. Molotov visited Berlin from 12 to 13 November 1940. At this point Nazi–Soviet relations hit rock bottom as Molotov flexed Soviet economic muscle and Hitler sensed impending blackmail. Historians have linked the Führer's final decision to launch Barbarossa with Molotov's visit.

In addition to lacking certain key natural resources, for which it was at least partly dependent on the Soviet Union, Germany had other weaknesses, which Hitler sought to offset to some degree with the Tripartite Treaty of 27 September 1940. Intended to build an anti-Soviet coalition and warn the US to keep out of Europe, the Pact of Steel only gave "the *image* of Axis solidarity" (Erickson/Dilks, p.87). Hitler did not, however, include his more senior Italian and Japanese allies in Barbarossa's planning, preferring instead to rely on his smaller eastern European allies.

Slovakia, grateful for independence from the Czechs, signed on early as a German ally. The defeat of France, her traditional patron, and her fear of Russia, pushed Rumania into the German fold. Ultimately she contributed more forces to Barbarossa than any other Axis partner. In recognition of German assistance in regaining territory lost in 1920, Hungary contributed a small contingent to Barbarossa.

By the summer of 1941 all of continental Europe, with the exception of the USSR, was Axis, Axis-occupied or neutral. However, the Soviet Union appeared finally to be awakening to the danger of its isolation. The United States stood securely beyond Hitler's reach. Between the outbreak of war and June 1941 the weaknesses and failings of her opponents had concealed the shortcomings of Germany's own military forces. The assumption, validated in previous campaigns, was that Blitzkrieg would only face an enemy's forces in being and that no opportunity would be given for the enemy to recover or rebuild.

German victories preceding Barbarossa undermined any legitimate German military opposition to Hitler. With his military and political position assured, Barbarossa was carried out according to the Führer's wishes. Army Group South's plunge into the great agricultural and industrial El Dorado of the Ukraine would satisfy all of the Third Reich's desires.

* * *

According to the Soviet interpretation of the Great War's beginnings, Russia had been tricked into attacking Imperial Germany in support of the western capitalists and had come out the big loser in 1918. Optimally Stalin would join any subsequent war only after comprehensive peacetime preparations and on his own terms. This meant waiting out the "self-laceration of capitalism and its fascist afterbirth (Nazism)" on the Western Front. But Germany's lightning victory in the summer of 1940 wrecked that hope.

In June 1941 the USSR was weaker, relatively, than its Tsarist predecessor had been in August 1914. Stalin's ruthless purges had decapitated its military in 1937–38, the five-year plans were losing momentum and by 1941 any potential continental allies had succumbed to the German steamroller. However, paramilitary organizations had trained over 13,000,000 snipers, radiotelephone operators, horsemen, vehicle drivers, pilots and parachutists. The Red Army grew to 5,000,000 men by the eve of Barbarossa. Significantly, the efforts of the Second and Third Five-Year Plans, which focused on heavy industry, were concentrated in the eastern regions of the USSR so that by 1940 37 percent of its steel, 35 percent of its coal and 25 percent of its energy production came from areas the Germans never reached.

In line with the secret protocols of the Molotov–Ribbentrop non-aggression pact of 28 September 1939 and exploiting Germany's distraction with war in the west, Stalin stole a march on Hitler in 1940, occupying the three Baltic states (Estonia, Latvia, and Lithuania) and Rumanian Bessarabia. In this instance, as well as at Khalkin-Gol in 1939, in the occupation of eastern Poland in September 1939[1], and in his war

1 See Campaign 107: *Poland 1939 – The birth of Blitzkrieg.*

against Finland in the winter of 1939/40 Stalin showed no hesitation in using the Soviet military. He levered economic power as well and, in seeking Stalin's help to circumvent the British naval blockade, Hitler became dependent on a very dangerous commercial partner. Stalin knew Hitler could not field his huge army without Soviet resources.

On the eve of war with Germany, however, the Soviet military was not in good shape. Like Mussolini's Fascist Italy, the Red Army had modernized too early, and by 1941 much of its equipment was effectively obsolete. In the early 1930s the Red Army had been at the forefront of mechanized warfare doctrine but nearly a decade later its attitudes were reactionary. During the Great Purge Stalin arrested and tried 9,506 army and air force officers (most were executed) and expelled a further 14,684 from service (although subsequently he reinstated many). The purges hit the higher ranks worst. The victims also tended to be the most experienced and farsighted of the Red Army's officer corps. The continuing executions and political interference from the kommissars undermined the morale of the remnants. The 1939–40 land-grab in eastern Europe pushed the Soviet frontier further west but deployed the army in unfamiliar terrain and left behind the old frontier fortifications. The lessons of Germany's Blitzkrieg victories were not effectively digested and applied to the Red Army's situation and fear of provoking Hitler further limited corrective action.

The key issue is not whether the USSR noticed Nazi preparations, but what it did with information received. Soviet generals informed Stalin of Hitler's 31 July 1940 meeting within days. Soviet rail passengers traveling through occupied Poland could not but see and report the massive military buildup. Numerous Luftwaffe reconnaissance planes crashed inside the USSR, their camera film full of photos of Soviet military facilities. Stalin's diplomats and spies, the British and others flooded Soviet intelligence agencies with detailed information of Germany's ongoing preparations.

Stalin made three critical errors of judgment that led directly to his nation's strategic, operational and tactical surprise. He believed, or perhaps chose to, that Germany was too dependent on Soviet resources to attack. He was further convinced that Hitler would not attack while the Anglo-American maritime powers remained intact on Germany's Atlantic flank and also that any invasion would be preceded by an ultimatum as had occurred with Czechoslovakia, Poland and indeed at the beginning of World War I. Nazi Germany had its "*Führer Prinzip*" and the USSR its "cult of personality." Institutional forces in each country and their respective philosophies contributed directly to the nature of Barbarossa. Approximately half an hour after German preparatory air and artillery fire began General G.K. Zhukov called the dictator with news of the attack. He asked "Did you understand what I said, Comrade Stalin?" Silence. "Comrade Stalin, do you understand?" At last Stalin understood.

CHRONOLOGY

1940

2 June Hitler tells von Rundstedt about eastern campaign.
18 June Halder sets up Eastern Front Study Group.
31 July Hitler briefs generals on his intent to invade USSR.
5 August Marcks completes his plan.
7 August OKW completes "*Aufbau Ost*."
October–May 1941 Luftwaffe aerial reconnaissance over the USSR.
Mid-October Stalin redirects Soviet main effort from Moscow to the Ukraine.
12–13 November Molotov visits Berlin.
28 November–3 December Paulus hosts Barbarossa wargames.
5 December Hitler approves basic plan.
18 December Führer Directive 21 issued.
23 December–13 January 1941 Kremlin command conferences and wargames; another shake-up within Soviet high command.

1941

31 January "*Aufmarschweisung*" adds Rumania to Barbarossa planning.
30 March Hitler describes Barbarossa to 250 generals as a "struggle of two world views."
6 April Germans begin Balkans campaign.
23 May Soviets call up 1905–1918 reservists, establish martial law.
30 May Mussolini establishes a corps for action in the USSR although Germans have not officially told Italy about Barbarossa.
6 June "Commissar Order" issued.
14 June Hitler clarifies Barbarossa objectives to Wehrmacht leaders: Leningrad, the Ukraine, Donbas and Caucasus. Moscow is not included.
20 June Rumanians first officially briefed on Barbarossa.
22 June ***Barbarossatag***; Soviet Military Districts become Fronts.
23 June Stavka created.
24 June First Panzer Group passes through Sixth Army; Kiponos' counterattacks begin.
27 June Unattributed bombing brings Hungary into war.
29 June 1st Mountain Division enters L'vov.
2 July Operation Munich crosses Rumanian border.
7 July 13th Panzer Division reaches Berdichev.
9 July 14th Panzer Division takes Zithomir.
10 July 13th Panzer Division reaches Irpen River, ten miles from Kiev, rest of III Panzer Corps close behind; Stavka creates Strategic Direction.
13 July Kirponos begins counterattacks against "Zithomir Corridor."
15 July 26th Army counterattacks at Kanev into First Panzer Group's rear.
17 July XI Corps crosses Dnestr River.
21 July Rumanians cross Dnestr; XLVIII Panzer Corps reaches Monastyrishche near Uman.
23 July Soviet counterattack at Monastyrishche.
27 July Seventeenth Army breaks free of Stalin Line, heads for junction with First Panzer Group.
30 July Sixth Army's first direct assault on Kiev.
3 August 16th Panzer and 1st Mountain Divisions link up at Pervomaysk, closing Uman pocket.
5 August Stalin fires Zhukov as Chief of Staff.
7 August 26th Army renews attacks at Kanev.

8 August Uman fighting over; Rumanians close on Odessa; Sixth Army's second attack on Kiev.

10 August Stavka gives up Dnepr River line.

16 August First Rumanian assault on Odessa.

19 August "LSSAH" takes Kherson; 9th Panzer Division gains bridgehead at Zaporozhe.

20 August Seventeenth Army wins Dnepr bridgehead at Kremenchug.

23 August 5th Army retreats behind Dnepr.

24 August Sixth Army reaches Desna.

25 August Soviets cut off Sixth Army (until 2 September); 13th Panzer Division takes bridgehead at Dnepropetrovsk.

26 August XVII Corps takes Chernobyl; Tyulenev replaced.

30 August OKH issues order for Kiev *Kessel*.

31 August Red Army abandons right bank of Dnepr.

7 September Sensing impending doom at Kiev, Kirponos requests permission to give up Desna line.

9 September Stalin approves Desna move; von Rundstedt orders Eleventh Army to attack Crimea.

10 September Sixth and Second Armies (Army Group Center) link up; 3rd Panzer Division reaches Romny; XLVIII Panzer Corps shifted to Kremenchug.

11 September Stalin fires Budenny, Timoshenko becomes commander of Southwest Direction.

12 September Von Schobert killed at Berislav.

13 September XXIV Panzer Corps takes Lokhvitsa; XLVIII Panzer Corps fighting for Lubny.

14 September 3rd and 16th Panzer Divisions link up at Lokhvitsa, completing Kiev encirclement.

16 September XXIX Corps' final assault on Kiev begins.

17 September Stalin permits evacuation of Kiev; von Manstein takes over Eleventh Army.

20 September Kirponos killed escaping Kiev.

23 September Soviet 9th and 18th Armies begin Sea of Azov battle.

24 September Kiev fighting dies down; LIV Corps begins first assault at Perekop (until 28th).

25 September Von Rundstedt orders First Panzer Group to counterattack behind Soviets at Melitopol.

29 September Oktyarbrsky suggests to Stalin that Odessa be abandoned.

1 October First Panzer Group attacks toward Melitopol.

2 October Rumanians renew assault on Odessa.

5 October Panzer Groups become Panzer Armies.

7 October XIV Panzer Corps and "LSSAH" meet at Berdyansk and close Melitopol pocket.

10 October Hoth replaces ailing von Stülpnagel.

15 October Soviets abandon Odessa at night.

18 October LIV Corps launches second attack at Perekop (through 26th).

21 October OKH orders Army Group South to Stalingrad and Maikop!

24 October Sixth Army takes Kharkov.

9 November Timoshenko briefs Stalin on Rostov attack plan.

16 November Eleventh Army reaches Kerch.

20 November III Panzer Corps reaches Rostov.

25 November 56th Army launches counterattack at Rostov.

27 November Timoshenko counteroffensive opens along entire First Panzer Army salient.

28 November Von Kleist orders III Panzer Corps out of Rostov.

30 November Von Rundstedt approves retreat to Mius River.

1 December Von Rundstedt resigns; von Reichenau named replacement.

2 December Hitler visits Army Group and Panzer Army headquarters.

OPPOSING PLANS

GERMAN PLANS

As indications of his confidence in his own military abilities and the importance of the ideological struggle against communism, Hitler put his mark on Barbarossa's operational details like no previous campaign. Taking into account the Army's and Luftwaffe's short striking ranges, the plan eschewed deep operations and settled on a line formed by the Dvina and Dnepr Rivers for its initial goal. As happened in Poland and the West, the Soviet's forward deployment played into the Germans' hands. Writing after the war former Field Marshal Friedrich Paulus recreated the contemporary mood of the German leadership: "tremendous vigor of National Socialist policy, then at its zenith" and "complete confidence born of the victory in the western campaign."

Erich Marcks wrote OKH's plan for Barbarossa then commanded the 101st Light Division. Shrapnel cost him his left leg on 26 June 1941. He died three years later commanding the LXXXIV Corps at St Lô.

Hitler began thinking of an eastern campaign before France surrendered. Initial planning began with the rushed (four days), poorly researched assessment of the Red Army's strength by Lieutenant Colonel Eberhardt Kinzel's *Fremde Heere Ost* (FHO – Foreign Armies East). All subsequent plans were based on the weak cornerstone of his inadequate and faulty analysis. With the German military focused on the Battle of Britain and Operation Sealion in the summer of 1940, Army Chief of Staff Colonel General Franz Halder gave responsibility for planning war against the USSR to Major General Erich Marcks, then Eighteenth Army Chief of Staff. One month later Marcks presented the *Oberkommando des Heeres* (OKH) his "Operational Draft East", which divided the invading force into three army groups with Moscow as the ultimate objective. Marcks' plan had three phases: I. the initial 250-mile push to the Dvina–Dnepr line; II. an intermediate phase consisting of a logistical pause and possible advance up to 100 miles; III. final drives on Leningrad, Moscow and the deep Ukraine.

Another lieutenant colonel, Bernhard von Lossberg, wrote the *Oberkommando der Wehrmacht* (OKW) plan largely on his own initiative. He also required only one month to create his *Aufbau Ost* (Buildup East). Both OKH and OKW assumed the bulk of the Red Army would be destroyed in Phase I. Von Lossberg's main contribution was to clarify Hitler's thoughts with regard to Phase II, specifically the turns north and south preparatory to the assault on Moscow that would prove the most controversial features of Operation Barbarossa. The drafting of the plans for history's greatest invasion had thus devolved on one major general – the *Heer*'s lowest general rank – and two colonels. All had drafted their plans based on the same questionable information so independent analysis and checks and balances were nonexistent.

Realizing that not only would Germany seek to secure the Ukraine's natural resources but also to put as much distance as possible between

Army Group South's ground-air team. Von Rundstedt and Lohr await Hitler's FW-200 aircraft at Uman on 28 August. Hitler visited Army Group headquarters one more time: in December to replace von Rundstedt.

Hungarian soldier with indigenous Solothurn 43M 7.9mm light machine-gun. Hitler's refusal to include Hungary in Barbarossa's planning and the resultant gap in the front caused Army Group South considerable consternation.

the Red Army and Rumanian oil, Stalin concluded the main effort would come in the south. Judging from his actions, Hitler as well as many German economic and military leaders, the *Abwehr* (counter-intelligence) and the *Heer*'s own Military Geography Department concurred. Planners in the OKH's Operations Staff favored giving weight to Army Group South in order to counter the Soviet main effort there. In fact, increased Soviet activity in the Ukraine in the winter of 1940/41 caused the Germans concern over operations in the south. Moscow beguiled many Army leaders, however, chief among them Franz Halder.

General Paulus, then Army *Oberquartiermeister,* hosted Barbarossa wargames between 28 November and 3 December 1940. Not surprisingly, they confirmed the primacy of the Moscow axis and a three-week Phase I followed by a logistical pause of the same length. Even at this early planning stage von Rundstedt asked for units from Army Group Center to attack southward into the rear of Soviet forces attempting to escape from Kiev. Army Commander Field Marshal Walther von Brauchitsch and Halder briefed Hitler on the wargames' outcome two days after their conclusion. The Fuhrer approved the basic plan. Significantly for Army Group South, however, he added a prophetic comment, declaring Moscow "not so very important." Hitler continually emphasized destruction of the Red Army in the field.

The OKW issued Fuhrer Directive No.21 on 18 December 1940 which, although it mentioned numerous geographic objectives, Moscow among them, clearly identified Barbarossa's main goal as the destruction of the Soviet military. Von Rundstedt was given three to four weeks to reach Kiev and the Dnepr crossings. He would then turn south to trap enemy forces against the Black Sea with the Caucasus oil region his ultimate destination.

Von Rundstedt had to cram the mass of his army group between the Rokitno Marshes and the Carpathian Mountains. He wanted to create a German–Hungarian force based on the Seventeenth Army, but Hitler distrusted Hungary and forbade any formal contact between the two militaries. Barbarossa underwent numerous revisions, including "*Aufmarschweisung* (Deployment Directive) Barbarossa" on 31 January 1941. This added Rumania to von Rundstedt's area of responsibility. However, the ensuing 200-mile Hungarian gap between Axis forces in occupied Poland and Rumania created numerous security, logistical and command and control problems.

Army Group South's original plan envisioned a double envelopment during Phase I, employing First Panzer Group in the north and Twelfth Army coming out of Rumania. Hitler soon decided against this course of action, and besides in April he ordered Twelfth Army to Yugoslavia and Greece. Eleventh Army took over duties in Rumania but these combined forces would not be ready by 22 June, giving Barbarossa its staggered start in the far south. Therefore von Rundstedt would fight mainly a frontal war, punctuated by occasional penetrations and (except for Kiev) relatively small encirclements.

One threat identified by FHO on 12 February consisted of Red Army forces that could retreat to relative safety east of the Rokitno Marshes, only to later attack the flanks of German thrusts making for Moscow or Rostov. This draft study anticipated perfectly the July and August controversies. Fearing dilution of his pet effort against Moscow, Halder deleted these

SS private and Unterscharführer attempt to cross a swollen stream with their field kitchen ("Goulash cannon"). Cooked food might be a luxury where campaign planners figured living off the land was good enough for the *Ostheer*.

references from the final version presented to Hitler on 21 January. The impact of Red Army elements lurking behind these marshes remained significant to Army Group South's operations, however.

Barbarossa suffered from a liability common to most Wehrmacht operations, namely the absence of a unifying strategic objective. The entire plan appears to be a combination of operational-level solutions to a war with the USSR. Traditionally directed at enemy forces rather than geographic objectives, the Germans therefore chased a moving target. These factors, with relatively weaker friendly forces and stronger Soviet forces, and a larger area of operations, combined to create difficulties for Army Group South. Additionally, von Rundstedt contended with a subtle prejudice within the Wehrmacht dating back to World War I when primarily Austria, not Germany, fought in the Ukraine.

Planners for Barbarossa have been variously described as suffering from "unbounded hubris" and "sublime inattention to logistical realities." But the *Führer Prinzip* then ascendant in Nazi Germany allowed no warnings, only optimism. It suspended reality, made the impossible feasible and substituted faith and will power for numerical strength and technological superiority. The invasion ultimately failed but first Army Group South would enjoy months of magnificent victories.

SOVIET PLANS

For at least a dozen years prior to Barbarossa the USSR vacillated between defensive and offensive strategies. By the late 1930s it built "fortified regions" along the border (the Germans called them the Stalin Line) behind which the Red Army would mobilize, fend off any attack and then launch a general offensive. In the Soviet experience static fortifications had been quite effective when used against them by the Finns, the apparent failure of the Maginot Line was attributed to specifically French weaknesses. The south played a prominent role in Soviet planning from a desire to ensure continued dominance of the Ukrainian people, retain the region's resources and industry and maintain a power base close to the Balkans.

During the 1930s Stalin used Soviet military leaders to expose traitors and saboteurs, not to improve the Red Army. German Blitzkrieg victories between September 1939 and June 1940 changed the world's military outlook. Red Army planning became more defensive – if only for the first few weeks of a future war. By October 1940 Stalin had ordered a change to an offensive orientation and a redirection of the army's main effort away from Moscow and towards the southwest axis. This became Mobilization Plan 1941 (MP 41) on 14 October and was further refined over the next six months. This commitment to an inherently, and excessively, offensive approach was not the USSR's only error: It assumed it would be forewarned of any attack by anything from "several days" to "not less than two weeks." In addition, although it knew Hitler had ordered the number of Panzer divisions doubled, it did not know that in order to achieve this the number of tanks per division had been halved.

Two Kremlin wargames tested MP 41 early the next January. In the first, Kiev Special Military District commander Zhukov led the Germans and won as expected; after all the Soviets had seriously neglected defensive doctrine. In the second Zhukov successfully defended the Ukraine and even launched a limited attack into Hungary and Rumania. His successes and high-visibility roles confirmed the primacy of the south in Red Army calculations. The day after the wargames' conclusion, 14 January, Stalin made Zhukov Army Chief of Staff but delayed making substantive changes in Soviet deployments for weeks.

When Zhukov took over as Chief of Staff he had only five months to implement a defensive strategy and minimize the offensive. Through April he updated MP 41 during a series of high-level conferences. New plans retained the need to hold the border, followed by an "active

German Pack Wireless Type d2 for company-battalion-regiment communications. Radios gave the Germans an advantage in command and control. During all of Barbarossa they captured only 149 radios from the Soviets, who relied excessively on the telegraph.

defense" followed in turn by a counterattack. This tactic consisted of allowing the Panzers to slip east then destroying each spearhead individually. His "Plan for the Defense of the State Frontier" issued the month before Barbarossa advocated a defense followed by an attack into the Reich's rear areas. Military Districts readied plans by April and distributed them to subordinate armies in May. Corps commanders were permitted to look through the plans, familiarize themselves with their general outline, but not to keep copies.

By spring Zhukov convinced Stalin to mobilize 500,000 reservists and send them directly to front-line units. At about the same time he and Defense Commissar Marshal S.K. Timoshenko learned of Barbarossa's final plans. They knew the Germans' *Schwerpunkt* was north of the Rokitno Marshes, yet Stalin insisted the Soviet emphasis remain in the south. To that end, Zhukov dispatched 19th Army from the Northern Caucasus to Tserkov (south of Kiev) and the 16th Army from Transbaikal to Shepetkovka in central-western Ukraine.

Despite Zhukov's changes no Red Army formations were fully prepared for the coming onslaught, the Southwest and Southern Fronts included. Kirponos' forces deployed too far forward in the First Operational Echelon, within 30 miles of the frontier. Bearing in mind its dearth of transport, the Soviet infantry would move slower than the Panzers attempting to bypass them, inviting disaster. Divisions within the many mechanized corps in the Ukraine were often based 100 miles apart from one another. Stalin Line fortifications in the south, approximately the Second Operational Echelon, generally ran between the pre-1939 frontier and the Dnepr. This massive river marked Kirponos' Strategic Echelon. Aware German forces in Rumania were separated from any support by Hungary, the Red Army planned to attack Hitler's ally once the initial assault had been blunted. Included were naval aviation raids against the Ploesti oil fields and amphibious attacks on Rumanian islands in the Danube delta.

At Zhukov's urging, the Red Army mobilized 303 divisions in the months prior to Barbarossa. The Soviet Union was finally actively preparing for war. As a testimony of Kirponos' good judgment, Soviet border guards fell under military command only in his Kiev Special Military District. Further in accordance with prewar plans, he planned to counterattack into the Reich, allocating two shock groups of three mechanized corps each, totaling 3,700 tanks for the purpose. The violence of von Rundstedt's assault overwhelmed these plans, however. As a final indication of the Ukraine's importance, on 22 June Stalin sent his best general, Zhukov, directly to the Southern Front's headquarters to coordinate its defense.

OPPOSING COMMANDERS

Von Kleist did an outstanding job leading his First Panzer Group (later Army) to Rostov. He wears the Knight's Cross awarded at the beginning of the 1940 campaign.

GERMAN COMMANDERS

Army Group South commander **Field Marshal Gerd von Rundstedt** enjoyed respect from friend and foe throughout World War II. Von Rundstedt was 65 years old in June 1941. During the Great War he had served on divisional and corps staffs. Twice superiors nominated him for the *Pour le Merite*. He commanded the Wehrmacht's main efforts during the Polish and Western campaigns.

After Barbarossa Hitler accepted von Rundstedt's resignation on 1 December 1941. In four months the Führer recalled him to command in northwest France. Frustrated and arguing with Hitler over the conduct of the fighting in Normandy, von Rundstedt again resigned. Two months later Hitler ordered him back to duty to command the Ardennes offensive, only to relieve him one last time in March 1945. Perhaps the worst black mark on his otherwise impressive career followed the July 1944 assassination attempt against Hitler when he presided over the cynically named "Court of Honor", which removed suspected conspirators from the Army to be tried by the People's Court.

Field Marshal Walter von Reichenau commanded the Sixth Army. He was 57 years old and had commanded this formation (named Tenth Army during the Polish campaign) for two years. Von Reichenau offered army assistance to Nazi Party elements purging the SA in June 1934, and authored the personal oath to Hitler sworn by all members of the Wehrmacht. Von Reichenau's men occupied Paris on 14 June 1940, and Hitler promoted him to field marshal the next month. After von Rundstedt's departure in December he additionally commanded Army Group South. He died of a heart attack in January 1942 while jogging in the Russian winter, becoming the first field marshal to die in World War II.

Colonel General Ewald von Kleist, age 60, led the First Panzer Group. He had served on the Eastern Front in World War I, fighting in the German victory at Tannenberg in 1914. Another long-time von Rundstedt subordinate, he commanded a Panzer corps in Poland and Panzer groups in France and the Balkans. In 1942 his First Panzer Army won a victory at Kharkov then raced to the Caucasus as part of Operation *Blau*. He defended first Kuban, then the Crimea and finally Rumania. He demonstrated expertise in both offense and defense. Von Kleist died in Soviet captivity in 1954, the only field marshal to do so.

Eleventh Army commander was the 58-year-old Bavarian **Colonel General Eugen Ritter von Schobert**. He stood firmly in the pro-Hitler camp during the interwar intrigues that dominated the *Heer*. He commanded the VII Corps in Poland and France. He was killed on 12 September 1941 when his liaison plane landed in a minefield.

General of Infantry Karl-Heinrich von Stülpnagel commanded the Seventeenth Army, having led the II Corps in France. **Colonel General Hermann Hoth** replaced him as Seventeenth Army commander on 10 October 1941. Actively opposed to Hitler since 1938, von Stülpnagel became entangled in the July 1944 assassination plot. He tried committing suicide in the aftermath of the plot's failure, but only managed to blind himself. He was subsequently tried and hanged on 30 August 1944.

A number of Army Group South corps commanders achieved notoriety. Soviet aircraft killed **General of Infantry Kurt von Briesen** of LII Corps southeast of Kharkov on 20 November. The Bavarian **General of Mountain Troops Ludwig Kuebler** was executed in Yugoslavia for war crimes in 1947. **General of Infantry Hans von Salmuth** served as Field Marshal Fedor von Bock's chief of staff in Poland and France. After commanding XXX Corps he led the Seventeenth, Fourth, Second and Fifteenth Armies.

Some of Barbarossa's division commanders also had interesting careers. Austrian **Lieutenant General Max de Angelis**, 76th Infantry Division, commanded his country's *Bundesheer* after the Anschluss with Germany in 1938. **Major General Ludwig Cruewell** gave up command of 11th Panzer Division on 1 September to take command of the Afrika Corps, only to be captured by the British on 29 May 1942. The 16th Panzer Division commander, one-armed **Major General Hans Hube**, was among the first Germans to reach the Volga River north of Stalingrad in 1942. As First Panzer Army commander he died in a plane crash the day after receiving the Diamonds to his Knight's Cross on Hitler's birthday in 1944. **Lieutenant General Hans Graf von Sponeck** initially led the 22nd Infantry Division. On 31 December 1941 General Erich von Manstein relieved him as XXX Corps commander for making an unauthorized withdrawal in the Crimea. Herman Göring presided over his court martial and the SS shot him on 23 July 1944.

Luftwaffe commanders included *Luftflotte 4* chief **Colonel General Alexander Lohr**. He served on the Austrian General Staff in World War I and prior to 1938 commanded the Austrian Air Force. He supported von Rundstedt in both Poland and the West and was in charge of all Luftwaffe forces during the 1941 Balkan campaign. After commanding *Luftflotte 4* in 1942 in the Crimea and at Stalingrad he became Commander in Chief South East. Yugoslavia executed him for war crimes in 1947. Lohr's principal subordinates from Poland through Operation *Blau* were World War I pilot **Lieutenant General Kurt Pflugbeil** (IV *Fliegerkorps*) and **Lieutenant General Robert Ritter von Greim** (V *Fliegerkorps*). Von Greim succeeded Göring at the head of the Luftwaffe on 26 April 1945, and committed suicide less than a month later.

SOVIET COMMANDERS

Marshal S.M. Budenny, aged 58, gained prominence as a crony of Stalin while commanding the 1st Cavalry Army during the Russian Civil War (guaranteeing his safety during the purges). After commanding the doomed South West Direction destroyed at Kiev he led the North Caucasus Front until relieved in September 1942. The following year Stalin appointed him to the largely ceremonial position of Commander of Red Army Cavalry.

Marshal Timoshenko (bending over) inspects a prewar defensive position while a lieutenant general and staff officers look on. Responsibility for halting Army Group South after the Kiev debacle rested on his shoulders.

Marshal S.K. Timoshenko was born in 1895. An NCO in World War I and another 1st Cavalry Army veteran, he oversaw the occupation of eastern Poland in 1939 and the climax of the war against Finland in 1939/40. Stalin thereupon appointed him Defense Commissar. Timoshenko initiated Red Army reforms in view of the early Blitzkrieg victories and had the unenviable job of preparing for Barbarossa. Considered the most competent prewar Soviet marshal, he commanded numerous fronts throughout the war and occupied Vienna in 1945.

Lieutenant General M.P. Kirponos ably led the Southwest Front through the battle of Kiev. He served in both World War I and the Russian Civil War. He rose to prominence when his 70th Rifle Division captured the Vyborg fortress in the closing days of the Winter War. Shortly afterwards Stalin rewarded him with command of the Leningrad Military District. As part of the Red Army command shake-up following the January 1941 wargames, Kirponos took over the Kiev Special Military District.

Lieutenant General I.V. Tyulenev commanded the Southern Front until wounded in September 1941. He was a cavalry officer in World War I and commanded a brigade in the 1st Cavalry Army. He presented a paper on defensive operations during the January 1941 wargames and subsequently commanded the prestigious Moscow District. On 22 June Stalin sent him and his staff to the Odessa Military District that two days later became the Southern Front.

In his post-war memoirs Zhukov singled out army commanders Kostenko, Muzychenko and Potapov for special praise. In 1938 the 5th Army leader, **Major General M.I. Potapov**, graduated from the Military Academy of Mechanization and Motorization. His skillful defense on the Southwest Front's northern wing created the salient in the Soviet lines that became the Kiev pocket. He later commanded the 61st Army in its defense of Moscow.

The 6th Army commander, **Major General I.N. Muzychenko**, had previously commanded the 15th Corps in the Winter War against Finland in 1939/40. Captured at Uman, he survived and returned home in 1945. **Major General F.Y. Kostenko** of the 26th Army went on to command a rebuilt Southwest Front in January 1942. He died in action near Kharkov four months later. **Lieutenant General Y.T. Cherevicenko** eventually succeeded Tyulenev and subsequently led the Bryansk Front near Moscow in early 1942 and the "Coastal Group" against Operation *Blau.* **Major General A.K. Smirnov** served as interwar Inspector General of Infantry and spoke on rifle division defense as part of the January wargames. He died in action when von Manstein crushed his 18th Army against the Sea of Azov in October 1941.

Two naval leaders excelled in land combat during Barbarossa. **Vice Admiral F.S. Okyarbsky**, Black Sea Fleet commander, was in charge of the besieged city of Sevastopol. **Rear Admiral G.V. Zhukov** (no relation of the Red Army Chief of Staff) ably commanded Odessa against the Rumanians. Both survived to command beyond 1942. Red Air Force commanders during Barbarossa were **Lieutenant General F. Astakov** (Southwest Front) and **Major General M.V. Zakharov** (Southern).

Some Mechanized corps commanders deserve mention: **Major General A.A. Vlasov** (4th Mechanized Corps), a Russian Civil War veteran, went on to lead the 38th Army in Moscow's defense and near Leningrad. Captured near Volkov in July 1942, he created the three-division-strong Russian Liberation Army, a force of former Red Army POWs. Vlasov was captured, tried for treason and hanged in 1946. The 9th Mechanized Corps commander, **Major General K.K. Rokossovsky**, was a World War I NCO and Civil War cavalryman who had been jailed during the purges. Later in the war he commanded the 16th Army, the Don, Central, and 1st and 2nd Byelorussian Fronts. After the war he served as Poland's Defense Minister. Within six months of *Barbarossatag* 16th Mechanized Corps leader **Brigadier General A.D. Sokolov** was promoted to Lieutenant General and commanded 2nd Shock Army near Moscow. **Major General N.V. Feklenko** of the 19th Mechanized Corps had served under Zhukov at Khalkin Gol.

OPPOSING ARMIES

Barbarossa's strain shows on this soldier's face. Following Uman, von Rundstedt's Order of the Day asked commanders to give their troops just one day's rest – after nearly two months of hard fighting.

ARMY GROUP SOUTH

Army Group South was a huge organization, initially consisting of 797,000 men in occupied Poland and 175,000 men in Rumania. On *Barbarossatag* von Rundstedt's command numbered 46½ German and allied divisions. Manpower and material shortages throughout the Third Reich meant that units varied according to when they were created. While most of Army Group South consisted of only German units on 22 June, the Eleventh Army had all-German corps and corps with Rumanians under command. During Barbarossa, corps' and armies' tables of organizations changed at a confusing rate.

All of the *Ostheer* can be divided into two groups; a motorized elite and the vast bulk of marching and horse-drawn troops. When, after the victory in France, Hitler doubled the number of Panzer divisions he robbed the German infantry of much of its motor transport. Lessons learned in that campaign, for example the benefits of motorizing both anti-tank guns and artillery forward observers, could not be applied to Barbarossa.

The greatest burden of the fighting fell on von Rundstedt's infantrymen – the *Landser*. Even the bulk of the Panzer divisions' combat soldiers rode to battle in trucks but dismounted to fight. As early as 22 June it became obvious that war in the USSR would be much harder that that in Poland or France. The 111th Infantry Division noted roads rendered impassible by rain as early as 24 June, while clouds of dust rose from the bone-dry steppe a day later. One company commander wrote: "the roads and the day belonged to the Germans. But the forests and the night belonged to the Russians."

Army Group South's armored formations were concentrated in the First Panzer Group. As a "group" it did not have the engineer, artillery, signals and other support units associated with an "army". After von Kleist's Panzer group became a Panzer army on 5 October it gained these assets. All of his Panzers were of German manufacture. The Germans hoped that newer Panzer III and IV would compensate for the smaller number of tanks in the reorganized Panzer divisions.

In modern warfare artillery usually causes the most destruction. At Army Group South's lowest level infantry platoons were equipped with 50mm and 82mm mortars. The campaign in the west had made clear that the former were too small to be effective. Larger formations had 105mm infantry guns and 150mm howitzers. Higher echelons fielded *Nebelwerfer* ("smoke projector") rocket launchers. These 150mm weapons threw an anti-personnel round over 7,600 yards. Von Rundstedt had four 280mm K5 railroad guns transferred from the English Channel. Each required two trains to move and operate and could send a 561lb projectile up to 37.5 miles.

Flak guns were critical to von Rundstedt's success, but when the Royal Air Force stepped up attacks on Germany Hitler ordered 15,000 army Flak guns held back to guard the Reich. Anti-tank artillery ("PAK") was stretched to the limit. German 37mm guns were useless against the new Soviet tank models, the 50mm gun only slightly better. Large-bore guns, normally used for indirect fire, operated against tanks over open sights. Luftwaffe Flak pieces, most notably the 88mm, were the *Landser*'s best hope of defeating Soviet armor. Germany never adopted the infantry-support tank used by other nations and instead employed the *Sturmgeschütz* ("assault gun"), which was employed in the infantry-support role.

Waffen-SS

Von Rundstedt Army Group included two SS formations – "Leibstandarte SS Adolf Hitler" (LSSAH) and SS Motorized Division "Wiking". Like all SS units in 1941 they consisted of volunteers drawn from the best of the German manpower. The "LSSAH" grew out of Hitler's personal bodyguard and was commanded by the Führer's crony, Sepp Dietrich. Throughout 1940 it grew from a regiment into a brigade and finally a division, although this reorganization was incomplete on *Barbarossatag*. "Wiking" was a full division, originally *Standarte* "Germania". Its uniqueness came from its Scandinavian and western European volunteers. Regiment "Nordland" hailed largely from Denmark and Norway while "Westland" was made up of Dutch and Flemish volunteers. Two SS *Einsatzgruppen* accompanied Army Group South to implement the murderous Nazi racial doctrine.

The Luftwaffe

After the costly Battle of Britain the Luftwaffe began Barbarossa with fewer aircraft than it had for the western campaign 13 months earlier. Army Group South air operations suffered from a number of handicaps: it was not the German main effort and so not fully resourced, it had no *Stukas* and many of its air assets were committed to the defense of Rumania's oil fields. *Luftflotte 4*'s close air support came from two *Gruppen* of Ju-88s and one fighter *Gruppe* fitted with ground-attack sights. Seven *Gruppen* of Bf 109s provided fighter cover while the II Flak Corps mainly protected Panzer Group One's spearheads.

In April *V Fliegerkorps* deployed to southeast Poland. It flew in support of the Sixth and Seventeenth Armies and von Kleist's Panzers. It covered an area 200 miles wide at the start and ultimately 900 miles deep, reaching to Rostov. The *IV Fliegerkorps* moved from France to Rumania in May. From there it supported the southern flank, initially against Bessarabia and the Crimea. Its front was approximately 350 miles wide and 300 miles deep.

Logistics

Barbarossa suffered from weak logistics from its earliest plans. These assumed the *Ostheer* would live off the land, in much the same way as had Napoleon's armies in 1812. OKH wargames recommended a logistics pause less than a month into the operation. Logisticians based Barbarossa's ammunition usage on the highest expenditures in the campaigns in the west – a flawed assumption. Separate and redundant supply systems for the army, Luftwaffe and individual allies added problems.

Horse-drawn artillery and limber at the XXX Corps' bridgehead at Berislav. The 105mm M18 field howitzer was the standard German divisional gun.

Soviet railroads had to first be cleared of Red Army units, and then German specialists converted the rail system to one they could use. Not only did the Germans have to change the rail gauge, a simple but manpower-intensive job, but Soviet signal facilities required modernization, Russian water stations were too far apart for smaller German locomotives and German coal had to augment the poor-quality Russian coal.

Truck transport between the railheads and the armies (the *Grosstransportraum)* and forward to tactical units was stretched to the limit. Poor convoy discipline caused further, self-inflicted hardships. A normal infantry division had 942 vehicles (not counting motorcycles) and 1,200 horses. Often augmented with hundreds of native *Panje* horses, these beasts carried most of the supplies. As Army Group South moved east and numbers of POWs mounted, many of these men volunteered to drive wagons, care for horses, handle supplies and prepare food. At times these "*Hiwis*" numbered up to 2,000 per division, or one-fifth of its strength.

Hungary

Hitler lacked faith in Hungary as a result of its weak support during the crises of 1938 and 1939. Therefore he forbade most military contact prior to Barbarossa. In the spring of 1940 Hungary volunteered to conduct mopping-up operations in Yugoslavia behind advancing German troops, alarming the USSR and linking Hungary to the Reich. Hungary joined the Axis on 27 June after supposedly being bombed by the Red Air Force the day before (in reality probably by Rumanian planes). It contributed a 24,000-strong "Fast Corps" under Lieutenant General F. Szombathelyi. Armored forces consisted of 81 indigenous "Toldi" tanks. Hungarian air contingents flew mostly second-rate German (He-112s) and Italian (Fiat C.R. 42s) machines. Hungarian forces first saw action on 9 July but played a steadily declining role. By November, obsolete weapons, high losses and a lack of enthusiasm led the Fast Corps to be withdrawn from the active front.

A 50mm Pak 38 in action at the Berislav bridgehead on 9 September. Its tungsten-core projectile could penetrate a T-34's armor and caused a redesign in the Soviet tank before the year was out.

Italy

Hitler left Germany's closest ally out of Barbarossa's plans; he wanted Italy to concentrate on the Mediterranean. Nevertheless, Benito Mussolini created the Italian Expedition Corps in Russia (C.S.I.R.), eventually under General Giovanni Messe, one of the few competent Italian generals to emerge from Albanian and Greek operations. Although technically taking orders from the Italian High Command in Rome, it initially came under the operational control of the German Eleventh Army. Italian Air Force units were subordinated to local Luftwaffe headquarters.

Individual Italian soldiers were undeniably brave but shared none of the Germans' crusading spirit. The Italians called their infantry units "auto-transportable", which the Germans wishfully misinterpreted as "motorized." This misnomer frustrated the Germans and upset the Italian troops, who marched everywhere! A mere battalion of L6/40 light tanks made armored operations difficult. Italian officers had minimal contact with their troops and each company possessed only six to eight NCOs. Of the C.S.I.R.'s 62,000 troops over 8,700 became casualties during Barbarossa (half of those were killed in action) and barely 4,000 ever returned to Italy.

Rumania

Rumania put its entire military at Germany's disposal for Barbarossa – the only Axis Ally to do so. In the Summer of 1940 she was in dire straits; Stalin grabbed Bessarabia, France and Britain were either crushed by Germany or struggling for self-preservation and finally Hitler and Mussolini awarded large tracts of her territory to Bulgaria and Hungary.

Huge petroleum reserves and a lengthy border with the USSR made Rumania indispensable to the Reich. The Ploesti oil fields provided one-half of Germany's needs. Occupying Bessarabia put Soviet forces only

ORDER OF BATTLE

Axis Forces – Army Group South area of operations[1]

ARMY GROUP SOUTH
FM G. von Rundstedt
Chief of Staff: Gen G. von Sodenstern
99th Light Inf. Div. – GenLt von der Chevallerie
Hoeh. Kdo XXXIV
4th Mtn. Div. – GenMaj K. Eglseer
113th Inf. Div.
125th Inf. Div. – Gen W. Schneckenburger
132th Inf. Div.

LI Army Corps
79th Inf. Div.
95th Inf. Div.

First Panzer Group – Col Gen Ewald von Kleist
13th Pz. Div. – GenLt F-W. von Rothkirch
16th Mot. Inf. Div. – GenMaj S. Henrici
25th Mot. Inf. Div. – GenLt H. Cloessner
SS Mot. Div. "LSSAH" – Obergruppenführer S. Dietrich

III Motorized Corps (Pz) – Gen Cav E. von Mackensen
14th Pz. Div. – GenMaj F. Kuehn
44th Inf. Div. – GenLt F. Siebert
298th Inf. Div. – GenMaj Graessner

XIV Motorized Corps (Pz) – Gen Inf G. von Wietersheim
9th Pz. Div. – GenLt Dr.A. Ritter von Hubicki
16th Pz. Div. – GenMaj H. Hube
SS Mot. Div. "Wiking" – Brigadeführer F. Steiner

XLVIII Motorized Corps (Pz.) – Gen Kempff
11th Pz. Div. – GenMaj L. Cruewell
57th Inf. Div. – GenLt O. Bluemm
75th Inf. Div. – GenLt E. Hammer

XXIX Army Corps – Gen Inf H. von Obstfelder
111th Inf. Div. – GenLt O. Stapf
299th Inf. Div. – GenMaj W. Moser
II Flak Corps – Gen O. Dessloch

Sixth Army – FM W. von Reichenau
LV Army Corps (Res.) – Gen Inf E. Vierow
168th Inf. Div. – GenLt Dr. Mundt

XVII Army Corps – Gen Inf Kienitz
56th Inf. Div. – GenMaj K. von Oven
62nd Inf. Div. – GenLt W. Keiner

XLIV Army Corps – Gen Inf F. Koch
9th Inf. Div. – GenMaj F. von Schleinitz
297th Inf. Div. – GenLt M. Pfeffer

Eleventh Army – Col Gen E. Ritter von Schobert
Rumanian Cavalry Corps (Res.) – Gen M. Racovita
22nd Inf. Div. – GenLt H. Graf von Sponek
Rumanian Defense: 72nd Inf. Div. – GenLt Mattenklott

XI Army Corps – Gen Inf J. von Kortzfleisch
76th Inf. Div. – GenLt M. de Angelis
239th Inf. Div. – GenLt F. Neuling
8th Rumanian Inf. Div.
6th Rumanian Cav Bde

XXX Army Corps – Gen Inf von Salmuth
198 Inf. Div. – GenMaj Roettig
14th Rumanian Inf. Div.
5th Rumanian Cav Bde

LIV Army Corps – Gen Cav E. Hansen
50th Inf. Div. – GenLt K. Hollidt
170th Inf. Div. – GenMaj W. Wittke

Rumanian Mtn. Corps – Gen G. Arramescu
7th Rumanian Inf. Div.
1st Rumanian Mtn. Div.
2nd Rumanian Mtn. Div.
4th Rumanian Mtn. Div.
8th Rumanian Cav Bde

Seventeenth Army – Gen Inf C-H. von Stulpnagel
97th Light Inf. Div. – GenMaj M. Fretter-Pico
100th Light Inf. Div. – GenMaj W. Sanne

IV Army Corps – Gen Inf V. von Schwedler
24th Inf. Div. – GenMaj H. von Tettau
71st Inf. Div. – GenMaj A. von Hartmann
262nd Inf. Div. – GenLt E. Thiessen
295th Inf. Div. – GenMaj Geitner
296th Inf. Div. – GenMaj W. Stemmermann

XLIX Mountain Corps – Gen Mtntr L. Kuebler
1st Mtn. Div. – GenMaj H. Lanz
68th Inf. Div. – GenMaj G. Braum?
257th Inf. Div. – GenMaj C. Sachs

LII Army Corps – Gen Inf K. von Briesen
101st Light Inf. Div. – GenMaj E. Marcks
Slovak Corps
1st Slovak Inf. Div.
2nd Slov Inf. Div.

Rear Army Area 103 – Gen Inf von Rocques
213rd Security Div. – GenLt l'Homme de Coubiere
444th Security Div. – GenLt Russwurm
445th Security Div. – GenLt Krantz

ARMY GROUP ANTONESCU – Gen I. Antonescu
11th Rumanian Inf. Div.
II Rumanian Corps – Gen N. Macici
9th Rumanian Inf. Div.
10th Rumanian Inf. Div.
7th Rumanian Cav Bde

Third Rumanian Army – Gen P. Dumitrescu
IV Rumanian Corps
1 x Cav Bn
6th Rumanian Inf. Div.

Fourth Rumanian Army – Gen N. Cuiperca
III Rumanian Corps – Gen V. Atanasiu
Rumanian Guards Div.
15th Rumanian Inf. Div.
35th Rumanian Res Inf. Div.

V Rumanian Corps – Gen L. Gheorghe
Rumanian Frontier Div.
21st Rumanian Inf. Div.

XI Rumanian Corps – Gen I. Aurellian
1st Rumanian Fortress Bde
2nd Rumanian Fortess Bde

Luftflotte 4 – Col Gen A. Lohr
Luftwaffe Mission Rumanian – Gen W. Speidel

Fliegerkorps IV – GenLt K. Pflugbeil
KG 27
JG 77

Fliegerkorps V – GenLt R. Ritter von Greim
KG 51
KG 54
KG 55
JG 3

Rumanian Air Combat Group
1st Bomber Wing
2nd Bomber Wing
2nd Fighter-Bomber Wing
1st Fighter Wing

1 No two sources on orders of battle for Barbarossa agree. The primary source for the order of battle for Army Group South is Horst Boog (ed.), *Germany and the Second World War*.

100 miles away. Both main authors of Barbarossa, Major General Marcks and Colonel von Lossberg, felt the country was essential for attacking Odessa and the Crimea and defending Ploesti. In November Rumania signed the Tripartite Agreement and German Army and Luftwaffe personnel in Rumania soon numbered 63,000. The Germans formally briefed the Rumanians on Barbarossa only two days prior to the start of operations.

Rumanian military reorganization took place amid political turmoil. The Rumanian army had previously concentrated on defensive doctrine using French methods where infantry and especially artillery benefited. German offensive doctrine and techniques were unfamiliar to the Rumanians and their armored forces struggled accordingly. Senior officers trained by the French resisted, while younger officers studied in Germany. Equipment consisted of a combination of purchased Czech, captured (by the Nazis) Dutch, loaned French, donated German, interned Polish and indigenous Rumanian – a maintenance nightmare. German training concentrated on the 5th, 6th and 13th Infantry Divisions and the Germans naturally considered these, along with the Frontier and Guards Divisions, the three cavalry and three mountain brigades, the most combat ready. They regarded Rumanian soldiers as resourceful and tough fighters with only modest needs. However, the Germans felt their allies' officers were corrupt and indifferent to their troops. Nevertheless, a former German general gave the Rumanian military credit for Barbarossa's successes. The German Military Mission became the Eleventh Army Headquarters in May and technically took control of all operations as soon as Axis forces crossed the Prut River on 2 July.

Two pilots with their Polikarpov I-153 fighter at a primitive airfield. Although the Luftwaffe destroyed many Soviet aircraft on the ground during Barbarossa's early stages their aircrews often survived.

Slovakia

Slovakia owed its independence in 1939 to Hitler. As part of the former Austrian Empire the Slovak military had some familiarity with German methods and German language. The Germans did not train Slovak units although some officers and NCOs went to Germany for military schooling. Slovakia contributed one battle-worthy unit to Barbarossa – Mobile Brigade (later Division) Pilfousek, numbering 132 tanks and 43 other armored vehicles. Germans considered Slovak officers indolent and lacking any concept of duty and their soldiers generally poor. By October they assigned even the Mobile Division only reduced missions.

SOVIET FORCES

Responsibility for defeating von Rundstedt fell to the Southwest and Southern Fronts. Zhukov praised Kirponos and his Chief of Staff Lieutenant General M.A. Purkayev and Operations Officer Major General I. Kh. Bagramyan for their "organizational skill and level-headedness." Kirponos commanded over 907,000 men. Three of his four armies and half of his eight mechanized corps defended the L'vov salient. Stavka created Tyulenev's command two days after *Barbarossatag* to fight in Bessarabia while giving Southwest Front freedom of maneuver on the critical Kiev axis.

Forces defending the Ukraine suffered from common Red Army weaknesses: 1) Inexperienced officers and NCOs – especially in headquarters. 2) Too few radios and too few qualified radio operators while communications for echelons above corps was telegraph – immobile and susceptible to Luftwaffe interdiction. 3) Logistics units were inadequate and untrained for their support missions. This despite the fact that 19 of 57 ammunition dumps, two of four fuel dumps, one of three repair depots and six of ten railroad regiments in the Red Army were in the southern theater.

Infantry represented the Red Army's backbone. The Wehrmacht acknowledged this before the campaign when it listed tough and brave

Soviet riflemen in hasty defensive positions. In one of the infrequent examples of good German intelligence they anticipated Soviet defensive capabilities, but even this did not prepare them for Barbarossa's harsh realities.

soldiers plus indirect-fire weapons (both defensive assets) as Soviet strengths. Army Group South's soldiers discovered through harsh experience that the Red infantry was "Panzersicher" (secure against Panzers). Prewar infantry divisions, of which Kirponos had 46, technically consisted of 14,483 men although in reality they had 8,000–12,000. Rifle divisions supposedly had a tank battalion, but earlier these had been absorbed into the mechanized corps. Both Southwest and Southern Fronts had an airborne corps. However, numerous airborne soldiers had made only one or two parachute jumps and many none at all.

By 22 June ten mechanized corps defended the Ukraine and Bessarabia. Prior to *Barbarossatag* German intelligence had identified only three so massed Soviet attacks surprised von Kleist's men. Unfortunately, the corps' subordinate units were spread over hundreds of square miles making concentration difficult. Poor readiness and conflicting orders further dissipated their strength. Army Group South faced as many as 5,465 tanks, although Soviet sources state that only 27 percent were in operational condition. "Older" BT-7 and T-26 tanks were better than Panzer Is and IIs and equal to some marks of Panzer IIIs and IVs. The T-34 and KV-1 tanks and the KV-2 infantry-support tank were superior to all German Panzers, about which the Germans had known since late 1940. Fully one-half of all Red Army tank losses resulted from poor maintenance, supply, driving and other non-combat causes.

The Red Army considered artillery its decisive branch. Kirponos alone fielded 16,997 indirect-fire weapons. Divisional guns were excellent models. The "*Katyusha*" (codenamed Guards Mortars) fired 36 82mm or 16 132mm rockets per launcher. They were cheap and easy to produce, terrified the Germans but suffered from inaccuracy and a slow reload rate. Anti-tank artillery represented a critical part of the Red Army's defensive doctrine. The standard 45mm gun could defeat all contemporary Panzer variants.

As the defender, the Red Army relied on earthworks and the Fortified Regions, each of the latter manned by a regiment with five to ten artillery

Soviet saboteurs captured after parachuting into Army Group South's rear near Uman. The German caption states they were subsequently executed.

bunkers, 10–15 machine-gun bunkers and 15–30 anti-tank bunkers. After March 1941 Kirponos put maximum effort into their construction, employing 43,000 workers per day. The Germans subsequently counted 1,912 completed, combat-ready positions and 192 under construction.

Red Air Force losses during the first days and weeks of Barbarossa are well known. Prewar Luftwaffe intelligence identified 38 air divisions, (120–240 aircraft each) and suspected the existence of 50 more. The Germans considered the IL-2 *Sturmovik* "an excellent machine" while the I-16 fighter possessed twice the rate of fire of the Bf 109 and fired a heavier projectile.

The Soviets dominated the naval war in the south. Against the small Rumanian Navy and a few German "E-boats", the Black Sea Fleet counted one old battleship, five cruisers, 17 destroyers, 43 submarines, numerous smaller craft and 624 aircraft. The Dnepr Flotilla had four monitors weighing up to 900 tons and mounting guns as large as 150mm, plus many gunboats.

Logistics troubled the Soviets as well. Trucks were at a premium despite the high production values of the Five-Year Plans. Mechanized corps' tanks attacked without their motorized infantry because their trucks were hauling supplies in the rear and many artillery pieces had no prime movers. Initially Kirponos and Tyunelev benefited from the highly developed Ukrainian rail system.

Some words on Ukrainian geography: Prehistoric ice sheets had scoured European Russia flat and shaped the Dnepr's watershed. Glaciers reached the Rokitno Marshes and created the low, water-saturated marshland. Elsewhere the soil was fine and humus-rich, producing particularly nasty mud that evaporated slowly. The *Rasputitsa* ("time without roads") ensued numerous times each spring and autumn as temperatures rose and fell and roads alternately turned into quagmires or froze hard as rock. The Ukraine lacked the vast forests found north of the marshes. It did contain numerous large rivers, the Dnepr being over a mile wide in many places. Interestingly, these rivers did not constitute a significant tactical barrier but hamstrung logistics – operations east of the Dnepr caused German rear echelon troops constant headaches.

ORDER OF BATTLE

Red Army – Southwest Front, Southern Front[1]

SOUTHWEST FRONT
LtGen M.P. Kirponos
5th Anti-tank Brigade

Front units
31st Rifle Corps – MajGen A.I. Lopatin
193th Rifle Division
195th Rifle Division
200th Rifle Division

36th Rifle Corps – MajGen P.V. Sisoev
140th Rifle Division
146th Rifle Division
228th Rifle Division

49th Rifle Corps – MajGen I.A. Kornilov
190th Rifle Division
197th Rifle Division
199th Rifle Division

55th Rifle Corps – MajGen K.A. Koroteev
130th Rifle Division
169th Rifle Division
189th Rifle Division

1st Airborne Corps – MajGen M.A. Usenko
1st Airborne Brigade
204th Airborne Brigade
211th Airborne Brigade

19th Mechanized Corps – MajGen N.V. Feklenko
213th Rifle Division
40th Tank Division
43rd Tank Division

24th Mechanized Corps – MajGen V.I. Christyakov
216th Motorized Division
45th Tank Division
49th Tank Division

5th Army – MajGen M.I. Potapov
1st Anti-tank Brigade

15th Rifle Corps – Col I.I. Fedyuninsky
45th Rifle Division
62nd Rifle Division

27th Rifle Corps – MajGen P.D. Artemenko
87th Rifle Division
124th Rifle Division
135th Rifle Division

9th Mechanized Corps – MajGen K.K. Rokossovsky
131st Motorized Division
20th Tank Division
35th Tank Division

22nd Mechanized Corps – MajGen S.M. Kondrusev
215th Mechanized Division
19th Tank Division
41st Tank Division

6th Army – LtGen I.N. Muzychenko
3rd Anti-tank Brigade

6th Rifle Corps – MajGen I.I. Alekseev
41st Rifle Division
97th Rifle Division
159th Rifle Division

37th Rifle Corps – BrigGen S.P. Zibin
80th Rifle Division
139th Rifle Division
141st Rifle Division

5th Cavalry Corps – MajGen F.V. Kamkov
3rd Cavalry Division
14th Cavalry Division

4th Mechanized Corps – MajGen A.A. Vlasov
81st Motorized Division
8th Tank Division
32th Tank Division

15th Mechanized Corps – MajGen I.I. Karpezo
212th Motorized Division
10th Tank Division
37th Tank Division

12th Army – MajGen P.G. Ponedelin
4th Anti-tank Bde

13th Rifle Corps – MajGen N.K. Kirillov
44th Rifle Division
58th Rifle Division
192nd Rifle Division

17th Rifle Corps – MajGen I.V. Galanin
60th Mountain Division
69th Mountain Division
164th Rifle Division

16th Mechanized Corps – BrigGen A.D. Sokolov
240th Motorized Division
15th Tank Division
39th Tank Division

26th Army – LtGen F. Ya. Kostenko
2nd Anti-tank Bde

8th Corps – MajGen M.G. Snegov
72nd Mountain Division
99th Rifle Division
173rd Rifle Division

8th Mechanized Corps – LtGen D.I. Ryabyshev
7th Motorized Division
12th Tank Division
34th Tank Division

KIEV V.V.S. – A.P. Ionev

19th Bomber Division
62nd Bomber Division
14th Mixed Aviation Division
15th Mixed Aviation Division
16th Mixed Aviation Division
17 Mixed Aviation Division
63rd Mixed Aviation Division
44th Fighter Division
64th Fighter D

SOUTHERN FRONT – Tyulenev

Front units
7th Rifle Corps – MajGen K.L. Dobroserdov
116th Rifle Division
196th Rifle Division
206th Rifle Division

9th Rifle Corps – MajGen V.A. Batov
116th Rifle Division
156th Rifle Division
32nd Cavalry Division

3rd Airborne Corps – MajGen V.A. Glazunov
5th Airborne Brigade
6th Airborne Brigade
212th Airborne Brigade
47th Rifle Division

9th Army – LtGen Ya. T. Cherevichenko
14th Rifle Corps – MajGen D.G. Egorov
25th Rifle Division
51st Rifle Division

35th Rifle Corps – BrigGen I.F. Dashichev
95th Rifle Division
176th Rifle Division

48th Rifle Corps – MajGen R. Ya. Malinovsky
30th Mountain Division
74th Rifle Division
150th Rifle Division

2nd Cavalry Corps – MajGen P.A. Belov
5th Cavalry Division
9th Cavalry Division

2nd Mechanized Corps – LtGen Y.V. Novoselsky
15th Motorized Division
11th Tank Division
16th Tank Division

18th Mechanized Corps – MajGen P.V. Volokh
218th Motorized Division
44th Tank Division
47th Tank Division

ODESSA V.V.S. – Gen F.G. Mishugin
20th Mixed Aviation Division
21st Mixed Aviation Division
45th Mixed Aviation Division

BLACK SEA FLEET V.V.S.
63rd Bomber Brigade
62nd Fighter Brigade

1 As with the Axis order of battle, the sources conflict on the details of Red Army organization. The primary source for the order of battle for Southwestern Front and Southern Front is David Glantz's *Barbarossa*.

OPERATION BARBAROSSA

FRONTIER BATTLE

A railroad engineer, here a lieutenant, contemplates a Soviet roadbed while a comrade keeps watch. Von Rundstedt had problems with *Reichsbahn* managers in the Army Group rear so put his staff officers in charge.

At 0300hrs on 22 June the last train out of the USSR crossed the San River at Przemysl into Greater Germany. From his new command post at Ternopol, Kirponos ordered units forward under the cover of darkness. Significantly these included the 37th Rifle Corps "training" in and around Przemysl. NKVD border troops moved from their barracks to their advanced positions. In Germany the Führer told his men "German soldiers! You're entering a hard struggle, heavy with responsibility. The success of Europe, the future of the German Reich, the existence of our people lays in your hands alone."

Main Axis

Reconnaissance troops of the 101st Light Infantry Division and commandos from Infantry Regiment 800 – Brandenburgers – rushed the Przemysl bridge over the San that morning. They failed in the face of alerted Soviet defenses but regular infantry secured the crossing later in the day. Further north the III Panzer Corps opened the invasion with a barrage by 300 artillery pieces. Opposite L'vov assault guns supported the 1st Mountain Division's attack against the 97th Rifle Division.

Kirponos reacted immediately by ordering the 15th and 8th Mechanized Corps against the XLVIII Panzer Corps. Their reaction was piecemeal; 8th Corps units were garrisoned up to 300 miles from the fighting. The Southwest Front put the 22nd Mechanized in motion while the commander of the 9th Mechanized, Rokossovsky, moved on his own

Rubber rafts of Infantry Regiment 222 crossing the Bug River on *Barbarossatag*. Many eastern European rivers were at high flood late into spring 1941, mitigating the significance of the delay caused by the unanticipated Balkan campaign.

initiative. Kirponos' best hope on *Barbarossatag* was parings such as the 87th Rifle Division and 1st Anti-tank Brigade at Vladimir-Volynskiy.

At 1300hrs on 22 June Stalin dispatched Zhukov to Ternopol. Luftwaffe air superiority meant he had to drive much of the way and didn't arrive until late in the night. Army Group South's relative slowness allowed him and Kirponos time to fine-tune their defenses. Fortuitously Zhukov gave Kirponos on-the-spot approval to the latter's counterattack plan to blunt the German assault.

Soviet riflemen and T-34 tank in the attack. Losses suffered by poorly conceived and executed attacks conducted as part of the Soviet strategy of the active defense meant any mobile counterattack forces would not be available later in the campaign.

During the second day, on von Kleist's critical right the 44th and 298th Infantry Divisions smashed a hole for the III Panzer Corps in the north along the Lutsk–Rovno axis while the 57th and 75th Infantry Divisions opened the way for the XLVIII Panzer Corps on the Dubno–Ostrog road to the south. However, between Vladimir-Volynskiy and Lutsk the 14th Panzer hit the 1st Anti-Tank Brigade and stalled. Only after the *Landsers* outflanked the anti-tank gunners did the Soviets conduct a fighting withdrawal closely pursued by the 14th Panzer.

On 24 June 4th Mechanized Corps assaulted the "Lucky" 71st Infantry Division's anti-tank battalion. Quickly reinforced by bicycle infantry the Germans waited. The first wave of 20 Soviet tanks got stuck in the marketplace of Niemerov, northwest of L'vov, where they could not fight well, maneuver effectively or retreat. Disaster awaited successive groups of ten or a dozen tanks until 50 sat destroyed or abandoned. On von Mackensen's right, arriving piecemeal, the 15th Mechanized lost ground against the XLVIII Panzer Corps. In all, during in their first major armor battle, von Mackensen's men destroyed 267 enemy tanks.

The following day the III Panzer Division forced the 27th Rifle Corps out of Lutsk and threw a bridgehead across the Styr River. Greim's *V Fliegerkorps* flew 1,600 sorties, attacked 72 airfields, destroyed 774 Soviet aircraft and interdicted untold convoys in three days. The 15th and 22nd Corps had been fighting since the 23rd and 24th respectively but were

Destroyed Soviet T-26 tanks at Ostrov, part of the counter-attacks Kirponos ordered in accordance with the Red Army strategy. A mere six miles separated his pincers but poor communications meant he knew nothing of his successes.

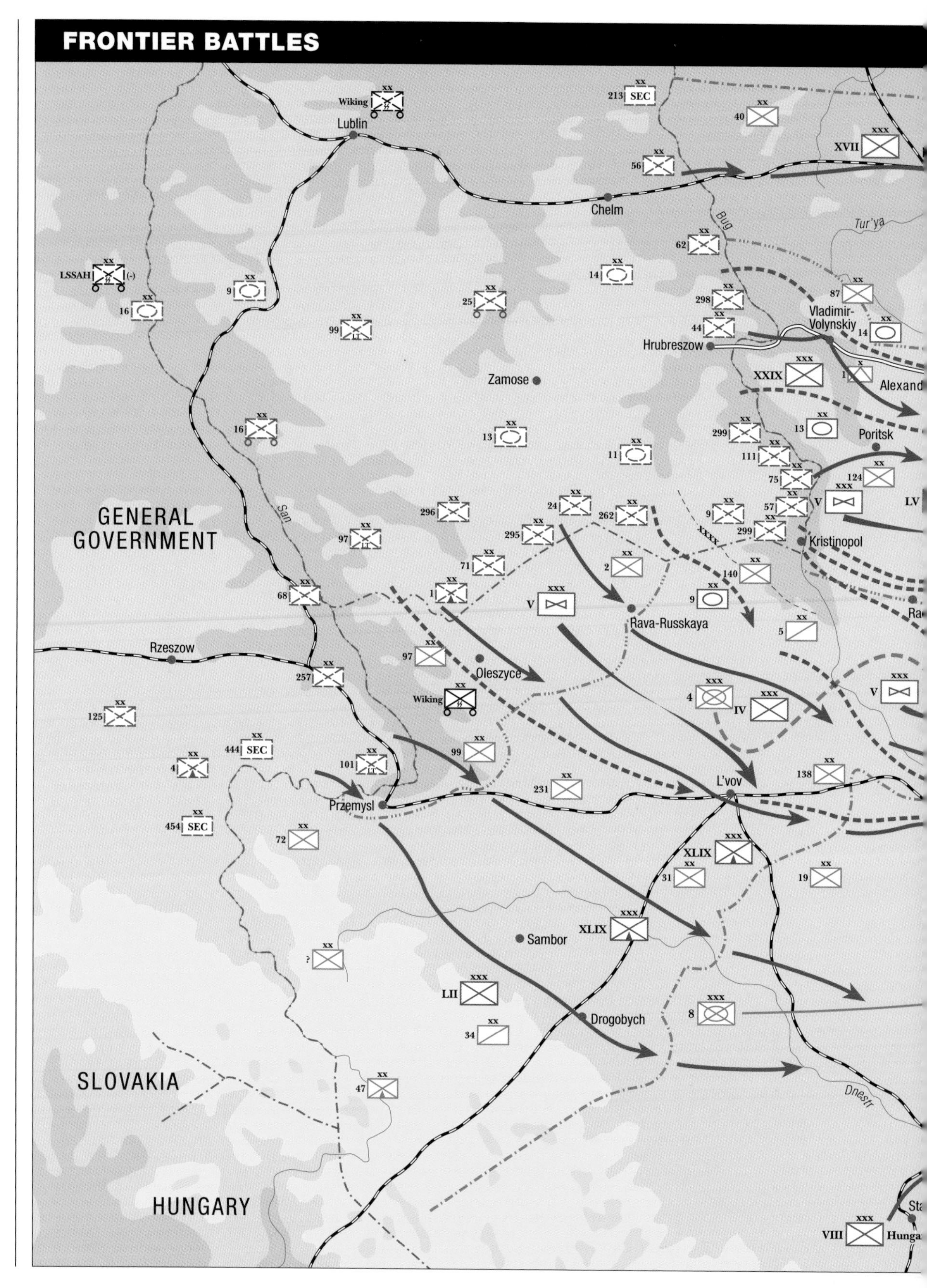
FRONTIER BATTLES
Lublin
Chelm
Bug
Tur'ya
Vladimir-Volynskiy
Hrubreszow
Zamose
Poritsk
Kristinopol
Rava-Russkaya
Oleszyce
Rzeszow
Przemysl
L'vov
Sambor
Drogobych
Dnestr
San
GENERAL GOVERNMENT
SLOVAKIA
HUNGARY
Wiking
LSSAH
XVII
XXIX
LV
V
IV
XLIX
LII
VIII
213 SEC
444 SEC
454 SEC

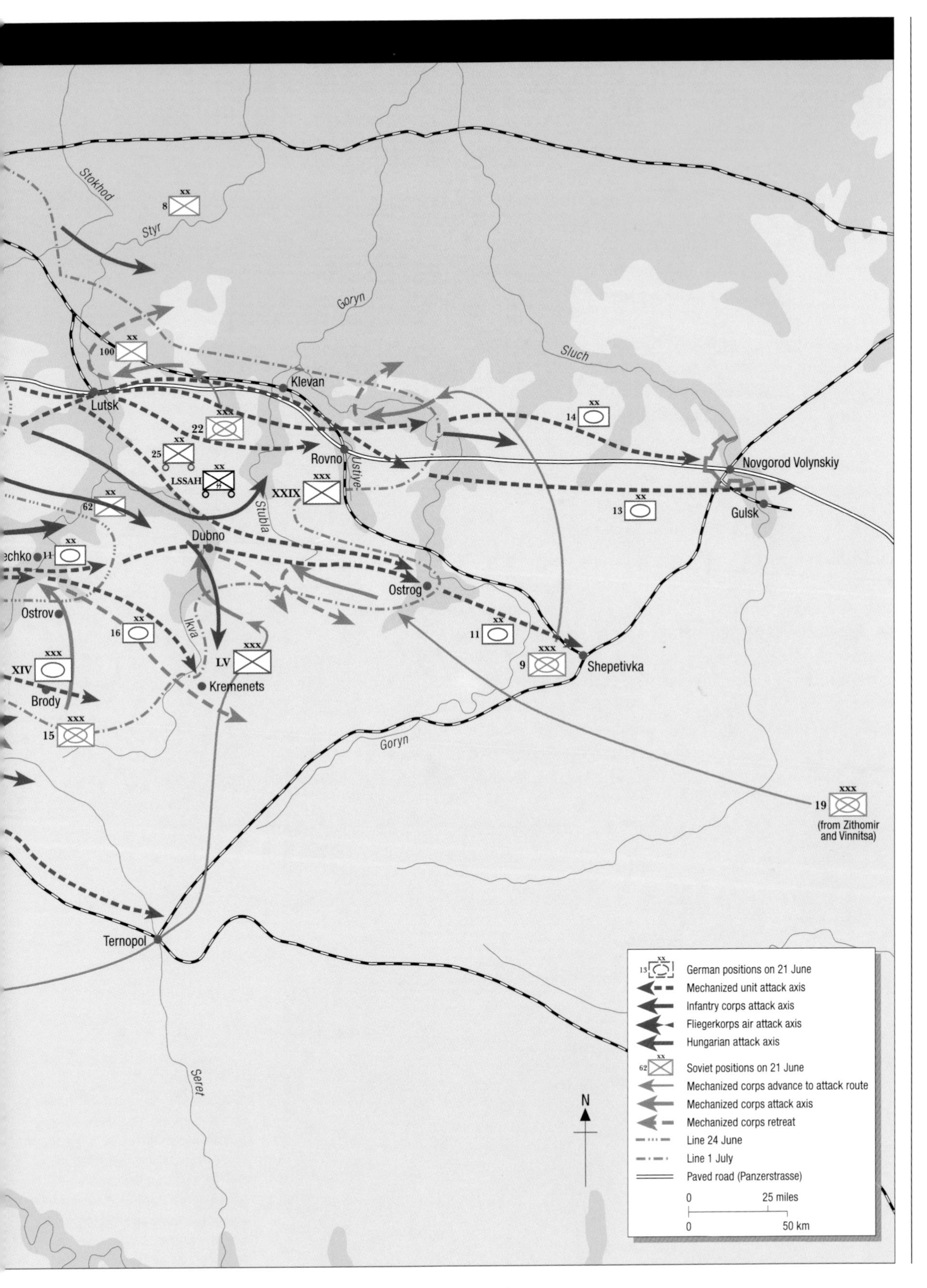

Stokhod
Styr
Goryn
Sluch
Stubla
Ustiye
Ikva
Seret
Lutsk
Klevan
Rovno
Novgorod Volynskiy
Gulsk
Dubno
Ostrog
Shepetivka
Ostrov
Brody
Kremenets
Ternopol
LSSAH
XXIX
XIV
LV
(from Zithomir and Vinnitsa)
German positions on 21 June
Mechanized unit attack axis
Infantry corps attack axis
Fliegerkorps air attack axis
Hungarian attack axis
Soviet positions on 21 June
Mechanized corps advance to attack route
Mechanized corps attack axis
Mechanized corps retreat
Line 24 June
Line 1 July
Paved road (Panzerstrasse)
25 miles
50 km
N

either decisively engaged or mired in swamps. Following march and countermarch covering over 100 miles the 8th, 9th and 19th Mechanized Corps arrived near the front, albeit at greatly reduced strengths mainly due to mechanical breakdown.

To simplify command and control Southwest Front placed the 9th and 19th Mechanized Corps under the 5th Army to the north. Their mission was to assault von Mackensen's left. The attacks lacked synchronization and the 13th Panzer defeated each portion in detail. The 1st Anti-tank Brigade halted the 14th Panzer again, however, this time near Klevan.

A German inspects a KV-2 helplessly mired in a swamp south of Ostrov in early July. Kirponos' counterattacks during Barbarossa's first weeks came to naught mainly due to incompetence and poor maintenance.

The Soviet attack on the south flank near Dubno began poorly when the Luftwaffe bombed the 15th Mechanized headquarters, wounding Karpezo. Soon it and the 8th Mechanized were holding their own against the 11th and 16th Panzer Divisions. The 8th, "reduced [by losses] to a manageable size" according to Rokossovsky, even worked its way behind the two Panzer formations. North and south pincers stood barely six miles apart with the 16th Panzer holding a division-sized *Igel* ("Hedgehog" defensive position) in-between. But initial gains abruptly fell foul of poor Soviet communications and mutual support. The 75th Infantry and 16th Panzer Divisions soon restored the German situation with Luftwaffe help. Kirponos heard only the bad news from the northern sector so called off his offensive.

He ordered his remnants to make one last attack on 30 June, but lacked sufficient strength. Political Commissar N.N. Vashugin, overruling the commander, personally led the 8th Mechanized Corps' tank division directly into a swamp, losing all tanks. Vashugin promptly committed suicide. Zhukov called the swirling battle around Dubno the toughest fighting in the Ukraine. First Panzer Group prepared to exploit the hard-won gap between the 5th and 6th Armies. Potapov fell back northward

Starting the spiral of genocide by both sides. Ten days into Barbarossa Germans discovered *Volksdeutsche* murdered by Soviet state police in L'vov. SS Division "Wiking" initiated a vengeful rampage. Pogroms by the Germans at Kiev and the Rumanians at Odessa followed.

A truck-mounted 20mm Flak 38 takes on a Soviet column. The truck's white "K" stands for von Kleist's First Panzer Group. An entire Luftwaffe Flak corps accompanied von Kleist.

toward the Rokitno Marshes, unfamiliar and uncomfortable territory for the Germans.

Von Rundstedt now worried that the Seventeenth Army lagged behind the Panzers. Until Axis forces in Rumania moved out, Army Group South labored with an exposed right flank. The LII Corps had the overall mission of protecting von Stülpnagel's right. It was here that Barbarossa's author, Erich Marcks, now commanding the 101st Light Infantry Division, suffered severe wounds near Prezmysl resulting in an amputated leg just four days into the campaign.

The 6th Army held a dangerously extended line, however. German signals-deception units in the Carpathians tied down many Soviet units needlessly along the Hungarian frontier. Musychenko resolved to hold L'vov. Although it initially didn't face any Panzers, this sector's defense possessed the 2nd, 3rd, 4th and 5th Anti-tank Brigades. At one point the German leadership considered pivoting First Panzer Group formations south to attack L'vov from the rear. Von Rundstedt would not hear of splitting his main offensive force. He feared a huge enemy logjam in L'vov that would defy either speedy maneuver or encirclement. Just then the newly committed 9th Panzer Division achieved a breakthrough and threatened the city from behind.

Kirponos decided on 26 June that his border fight was over and began to withdraw on the 27th. Two days later the 1st Mountain Division occupied L'vov without a fight. To cover the retreat Vlasov's 4th Mechanized Corps counterattacked to regain the city the next day. At times German and Red Army troops were only paces apart. In the cemetery 71st Infantry Division *Landsers* fought from headstone to headstone.

On 1 July SS Division "Wiking" took up the pursuit but the Soviet withdrawal went smoothly. The Hungarian VIII Corps took the field on the 2nd, crossing the Dniester near Stanislav. The Seventeenth Army had ripped a 20-mile hole between the 6th and 26th Armies. Von Rundstedt pushed his men to occupy the Stalin Line before the Red Army could. Kirponos instructed his men to occupy the Stalin Line by 9 July.

Back in the northern portion of the sector von Kleist's tankers spread out with the 11th Panzer in the lead. First Panzer Group had destroyed

Having just broken through the Stalin Line, *Landsers* hitch a ride aboard an assault gun. The defensive fortifications were of uneven quality, offering little resistance at one point or delaying the Germans for days elsewhere.

1,200 Soviet tanks in about ten days. Southwest Front's initial armored vehicle superiority dwindled; Red Army tank losses were permanent while the Germans, in possession of the battlefields, recovered and repaired damaged Panzers. During the same period Red Air Force elements supporting Kirponos admitted to losing a similar number of aircraft. Its commander, Major General Ptukhin, a Spanish Civil War veteran, was relieved on 1 July and executed.

The Stalin Line

Thus far the Southwest Front's performance far surpassed the bulk of the Red Army. Kirponos avoided allowing a penetration of his lines and though out-classed, kept the enemy squarely to his front. But as his defenses fell back its frontage increased from just over 500 miles on *Barbarossatag* to nearly 850 miles at the end of June. However, by occupying the old Polish-Soviet border Kirponos in turn reduced his front by 200 miles. The permanent defenses that awaited Kiponos' men there were described by von Stülpnagel to his troops as "like the Westwall," which was falsely flattering to both lines. By 4 July, however, the Soviet defense had lost all cohesion and the Germans stood in the midst of the fortified region near Novgorod-Volynskiy.

Von Rundstedt issued his Order No.2 on 28 June, initiating the race for the Stalin Line. In the lead, von Mackensen's Panzer divisions oriented southwards and boldly planned to penetrate the obstacle. In places 210mm mortars were required to break the line. Soviet artillery, anti-tank and anti-aircraft guns cooperated to good effect. One company of the 16th Panzer Division lost three successive company commanders in two hours of tough fighting. While the 13th Panzer had an easier time of it near Gulsk, the 14th Panzer struggled near Novgorod-Volynsky. The 25th Motorized maintained contact between the two. The *V Fliegerkorps* provided close-air support, its fighters keeping the skies free of Red Air Force interference. The 13th Panzer reached Berdichev by 7 July while the 14th Panzer took Zithomir and its stout bunker line two days later. Von Kleist finally had freedom to maneuver. He sent the III Panzer Corps "to occupy Kiev as a deep bridgehead east of the Dnepr," the XIV Panzer Corps through Fastov to Balaya Zerkov and the XLVIII Panzer Corps toward Kasatin.

The Soviets reacted quickly. On 7 July Zhukov ordered Southwest Front to attack Berdichev while on the 9th Kirponos dispatched 5th Army to Broniki and Chenitsa. As usual, internal conflict now distracted the German high command. On 9 July Hitler advocated splitting the First Panzer Group into corps. He wanted it to both head for Kiev and seek an encirclement inside the Dnepr bend. OKH and army group leaders opposed the move, wanting to leave the city to the Sixth Army's infantrymen. The Führer remained focused on destroying enemy forces and issued orders to trap the Soviets near Vinnitsa. Two events rendered the argument moot. First, the 13th Panzer reached and then crossed the Irpen River; 20 miles from Kiev, they stood among the city's first line of defense. Secondly, Stavka created a new echelon of command, the "Strategic Direction", and appointed Marshal Budenny to oversee the efforts of the Southwest and Southern Fronts plus the Black Sea Fleet. The offensive-minded marshal and his Political Commissar, N.S. Khrushchev, ordered vigorous counterattacks against the German spearheads.

The 13th Panzer stood nearly 70 miles in front of the bulk of von Mackensen's corps still near Zithomir. The III Panzer Corps had bisected Kirponos' force; henceforth the 5th Army held north of Kiev while the 6th and 12th Armies slipped to the south. To rectify this situation Budenny ordered forward the remainder of the mechanized forces with the 16th, 18th, 19th and 62nd Air Divisions flying overhead. The 9th (down to 64 tanks), 19th and 22nd (30 tanks each) Mechanized Corps continued attacking von Reichenau in the north while the 4th, 15th and 16th struck near Berdichev. Keeping the 13th Panzer supplied became problematic as heavy fighting raged to the Panzer Group's rear between 13 and 18 July. The 14th Panzer Division defended Makarov as the 25th Motorized – battling nine rifle divisions – held near Zithomir with the recently assigned "LSSAH".

Kirponos' 5th and 6th Armies maintained pressure against this "Zithomir corridor." Von Rundstedt threw in reinforcements and *Stukas.*

Regimental command post at an abandoned Stalin Line bunker near Kiev. A lieutenant colonel points at his map as signalmen wait by their Pack Wireless Type d2 to transmit either by voice or Morse Code. The communications net of the German forces was vastly more extensive and robust than that of the Red Army.

An assault gun of StuG Abteilung 191 at Malin is resupplied by a halftrack one month into Barbarossa. Assault guns were intended to help infantry reduce fortifications and force river crossings, but were also employed fighting enemy tanks. StuG Abteilung 191 was nicknamed the Buffalo battalion after its unit emblem. It was established following the campaign in France and fought in the Balkans prior to Barbarossa. It remained deployed on the Eastern Front, ending the war as StuG Brigade 191 in Hungary.

Red Army artillery halted numerous attacks while rifle regiment strength sank to 300 men. Budenny's counterattacks foundered due to material weakness not lack of enthusiasm. At Berdichev his men made human-wave assaults without the benefit of heavy weapons. The 11th Panzer Division suffered 2,000 casualties in these battles alone. With the help of Sixth Army's infantry a route to the 13th Panzer opened on the 19th. But Soviet resistance caused a critical expenditure of time and material. The First Panzer Group could no longer turn southwest to Vinnitsa, but would have to drive directly south to Uman. As for Kirponos, his defense in the southern theater henceforth would have to rely on the broad Dnepr and surviving Red artillery.

North of Kiev von Reichenau kept the pressure on the 5th Army, which nevertheless retired in good order. Von Kleist turned south toward the intended encirclement at Uman. This move also created a gap generally south of Kiev. To fill the void von Rundstedt created an *ad hoc* army of six (later nine) infantry divisions named Group Schwedler (named after the IV Corps commander). Seventeenth Army pushed southeast but faltered mainly due to the weather and mud. Kirponos sensed the growing threat, recognized the Germans were about to outmaneuver him and ordered a general withdrawal from the Vinnitsa area.

Von Stülpnagel finally punched through the Stalin Line in mid-July. On the 18th the 1st Mountain Division with *Sturmgeschütz* support took a Bug River bridge close to Vinnitsa. After coming up empty-handed at L'vov Hitler saw an opportunity to trap over 50,000 Soviets. Along with the 4th Mountain and 24th Infantry Divisions, the 1st Mountain tried to close the pocket. With von Kleist's Panzers still far off to the north and east and the Eleventh Army slowed to the south the cordon was too thin, however, and Red Army forces escaped as Kirponos had ordered. Hitler paid dearly for his spiteful decision to not include Hungary in Barbarossa's initial planning. Destruction was postponed not escaped as the 6th and 12th Armies slipped southeastwards, however. The day before they retreated over the Bug Hitler ordered another, even larger encirclement near Uman.

The Rumanian Front

In April the 170th Infantry Division made a 17-day train trip to Rumania to join other Germans to guard the Ploesti oil fields. They reconnoitered the Soviet border in civilian clothes and trained Rumanian units. After *Barbarossatag* the Red Air Force launched hundreds of attacks against the oil facilities without success. Hitler finally felt chances of a Soviet ground attack were low enough that his far right flank could move out under Operation Munich.

All Axis forces in Rumania nominally fell under the command of dictator Ion Antonescu. But von Schobert's staff conducted most planning while *de facto* controlling the Rumanian Third Army. The *IV Fliegerkorps* provided close air support. To the south the Rumanian Fourth Army initially guarded the Black Sea coast and lower Prut. As for the Soviets, Tyulenev left Moscow on 22 June and arrived at Southern Front headquarters at Vinnitsa two days later. He found no phones, telegraphs or radios. But he had one week longer than the rest of the Red Army to prepare.

Prior to Operation Munich, Army Group South was constricted between Army Group Center and Hungary. But when von Schobert got under way the area the Soviets had to defend tripled. To avoid detection, prior to attacking German soldiers bivouacked by day and marched toward the border by night. On the evening of 30 June, 46 men of Infantry Regiment 399 stormed a 300-foot bridge over the Prut, and took it without a shot. The Soviets counterattacked and by the next morning half the Germans were dead but their bridgehead remained.

Von Schobert's main offensive began on 2 July from these bridgeheads on either side of Iassy while assault boats crossed the Prut at 0315hrs. Eleventh Army struck the boundary between the 9th and 18th Armies, where the Soviets were not fully prepared. Fighting centered around Beltsa where the XXX Corps tangled with the 48th Rifle Corps and at Kishinev, taken by the Fourth Army. Farthest north, where the distance between the Prut and Dniestr Rivers was smallest, the XI Corps and Rumanian Cavalry and Mountain Corps closed in on the

A destroyed bridge over the Bug River at Vinnitsa. Von Rundstedt's first encirclement opportunity slipped away at Vinnitsa when the Seventeenth Army's marching infantry could not close the trap alone in the face of Soviet resistance and demolitions.

Operation Munich. Rumanian cavalry crossing the Prut River to reoccupy Moldavia. Employed in brigade-sized divisions, cavalry units were among Rumania's best troops.

latter watercourse at Mogilev-Podol'skiy. Attempts to gain a bridgehead by *coup de main* failed when XI Corps could not negotiate the 45-mile gap and relieve the company of Brandenburgers. These commandos managed to hang on only for a few hours before being overwhelmed. Southern Front's Dniestr line remained intact, a fact that had long-term negative effects on German operations until Uman.

Simultaneously Tyulenev took two defensive measures: he created a counterattack force of 2nd Cavalry, 2nd Mechanized and 48th Rifle Corps to reconquer Kishinev, and; he created a "Coastal Group" of three rifle divisions to cover the lower Prut. The Kishinev offensive struck the boundary of Eleventh and Rumanian Fourth Armies. Originally Barbarossa's plan called for the assignment of the XIV Panzer Corps to Eleventh Army. But Hitler reversed this decision, leaving von Schobert vulnerable to Soviet armor. The assault soon foundered but not before scattering the Rumanians and forcing von Schobert to dispatch the LVI Corps to shore them up.

Meanwhile German pressure on the Moscow axis had a negative effect on operations in the south. As part of the northward migration of Red Army units Stavka ordered Tyulenev to transfer the 7th Rifle Corps (116th, 196th and 227th Rifle Divisions) north to the Southwest Front while Kirponos lost the 16th and 19th Armies to the Western Front. On 16 July Budenny ordered Tyulenev to evacuate the Dniester and on the next day instructed him to mass near Uman. This played directly into von Rundstedt's hands. The Eleventh Army now planned its own encirclement between the Dniester and Bug Rivers. Von Schobert ordered his left – XI Corps, Rumanian Third Army and the arriving Italians – to swing clockwise along the west bank of the Bug and behind Tyulenev.

The XI Corps began a deliberate crossing of the Dnestr on 17 July. The steep slopes and thick woods reminded the Germans of their own Mosel valley. *Stukas* provided close air support, assault guns fired from the near bank while 88mm Flak guns destroyed Soviet bunkers across the river. They succeeded this time against limited resistance and the

XI, XXX Corps and Rumanian Cavalry and Mountain Corps crossed over by the 21st. Further south the LIV Corps, having just fought its way through Kishinev, lagged behind.

Poor weather and Soviet scorched-earth policies slowed the Axis forces, allowing the Southern Front to escape. Arriving on the *Ostfront* to great fanfare, the Italian Expeditionary Corps experienced its baptism of fire. Its commander, General Messe, consolidated his transport for the "Pasubio" Division. This unit bore the brunt of the fighting while the now un-motorized "Torino" marched far to the rear. "Pasubio" earned von Schobert's praise during the battles between the Dnestr and Bug Rivers. Tyulenev's 18th Army had a difficult time fighting its way rearward; the Luftwaffe destroyed bridges over the numerous waterways, Soviet pioneers rebuilt them for their retreating comrades, then attempted to demolish them again to deny their use to the advancing Axis troops. Tyulenev eventually escaped, denying the Eleventh Army its own *Kessel.*

* * *

General Herman Hoth credits Kirponos' resistance on the border for denying von Rundstedt the same breakthroughs enjoyed by Army Groups North and Center. The battles around Dubno and Rovno held up von Rundstedt for at least one critical week. This hard-won delay represented a double-edged sword, however: once the frontier battles concluded little organized resistance stood in Army Group South's way. In addition, Soviet prewar offensive doctrine had succeeded in fixing Red Army forces too far forward, leaving untrained armor at the mercy of the Panzers and making withdrawal difficult. Forces defending along the Kiev axis proved inadequate to hold von Kleist while elements in the

A rubber raft, in this case a "Grosser Flossack", used to cross the Ukraine's many rivers. The troops appear to be Gebirgsjäger with the soldier in front carrying a Panzerbüchse 39, the infantry's standard anti-tank weapon. It's 7.92mm round proved ineffective against most Soviet tanks.

A weary Italian foot column with pack mules. Soldiers on the near side of the road seem to be regular infantry. Those on the far side are *Bersaglieri* (light infantry) with black cockerel feathers in their helmets.

south counterattacked into Rumania according to the prewar plan. The unexpected severity of Luftwaffe interdiction and the evacuation of Ukrainian industry upset Zhukov's plans for coordinated operational-level counteroffensives. With minor interruptions Axis forces advanced east. Even then the Red Army still possessed considerable powers of resistance.

UMAN AND THE FLANKS

Hitler had high expectations now that Army Group advanced beyond the Stalin Line. Operations were disjointed as usual while the German high command solved problems remaining from the initial ambiguities of Führer Directive 21. While Hitler wanted to split up First Panzer Group for a number of objectives von Rundstedt argued for its continued concentration. Hitler sought a quick capture of Kiev (i.e. by von Kleist) while the field marshal wanted to leave the fortified city to the Sixth Army. Halder simply craved progress on the flank army groups that would dissuade the dictator from weakening the Moscow axis.

Von Rundstedt's men achieved two breakthroughs, First Panzer Group slicing toward Kiev and Seventeenth Army aiming south of Vinnitsa. Stavka encountered difficulty discerning Barbarossa's geographic objectives because there weren't any: Army Group South's goal was the destruction of the Red Army – a moving target. Kirponos maintained an intact defense but positive control of the Southwest Front slipped from his grasp. His 6th and 12th Armies fell southward into the Southern Front's area of operations. Meanwhile the 5th Army slid further north into the Rokitno Marshes.

Identified from Barbarossa's inception but downplayed by German planners, this massive terrain feature now demanded a solution. The marshes are often mislabeled a swamp. It is a primeval forest, primarily deciduous trees. Low areas are bogs while the high ground is covered with pine trees. The Soviets wanted to capitalize on the marshes' defensive benefits as much as the Germans hoped the problem would go away.

A month into Barbarossa, von Reichenau found his Sixth Army in a very awkward position. When von Kleist sliced through, creating his own front, he split the Sixth Army. The southern portion was task-organized into Group Schwedler while the northern units remained under von Reichenau. But the field marshal was not up to the task; in one of the Wehrmacht's best-kept secrets, von Reichenau had suffered a "light stroke" the winter before and he would be dead of another the winter after.

Potopov's 5th Army, separated from the bulk of Kirponos' forces, avoided decisive engagement and sniped at the Sixth Army from the relative safety of the marshes. German intelligence failures contributed to the Sixth Army's discomfort by inflating the enemy, never larger than twelve divisions, to nearly 20. The Soviet 5th Army launched disrupting attacks as the Red Air Force lavished attention on exposed German units. Together they succeeded in keeping von Reichenau distracted from his main objective – Kiev.

Kiev

Even with his lines of communication through the "Zithomir corridor" cut, von Kleist focused on the Ukrainian capital. By 10 July the 13th Panzer Division soldiers could see the Kremlin spires. The 14th Panzer pulled alongside the next day. Soon the 25th Motorized Division joined them, making a solid line on the Irpen River, barely ten miles from the city. Knowing infantry and artillery support necessary for the traditional assault was 100 miles to the rear, the decision of whether or not to take the city by *coup de main* rested with von Mackensen.

The Irpen is a small river with up to ⅔ mile of swamp on either bank, representing quite an obstacle to his Panzers. Initially Khrushchev commanded the garrison, a collection of regular infantry equal to three rifle divisions, an airborne brigade, a tank regiment, NKVD motorized forces, the 1st Kiev Artillery school, two anti-tank battalions and approximately 29,000 militia. At an 11 July meeting Kirponos concluded First Panzer Group had the mission of taking Kiev. Almost simultaneously Hitler halted von Kleist and prohibited a direct assault on the increasingly heavily defended city. At army group headquarters von Brauchitsch added his belief that the Panzers could not both take the city and execute the Uman *Kessel*. Von Rundstedt concurred while von Reichenau compared the proposed city fight to Verdun.

The marching infantry of the Sixth Army finally broke through the Stalin Line and by late July approached Kiev. They relieved III Panzer Corps on siege duty, work made difficult by heavy Soviet artillery fire. The Uman encirclement now required the attention of von Mackensen's men. Von Reichenau could expect little assistance from army group and any help from Army Group Center, fighting for Smolensk, was unlikely.

Uman

When the Panzers pulled out of the Kiev line Kirponos thought he had succeeded in blunting the German' assault. He did not realize von Kleist had swung south toward Uman. The Germans had decided on this less-ambitious pocket instead of following the great bend in the Dnepr.

Splitting the 5th and 6th Armies even further apart, First Panzer Group pivoted on Belaya Zerkov. Kirponos ordered all his air assets in this direction. Although it took nearly a week, Stavka finally saw the threat to

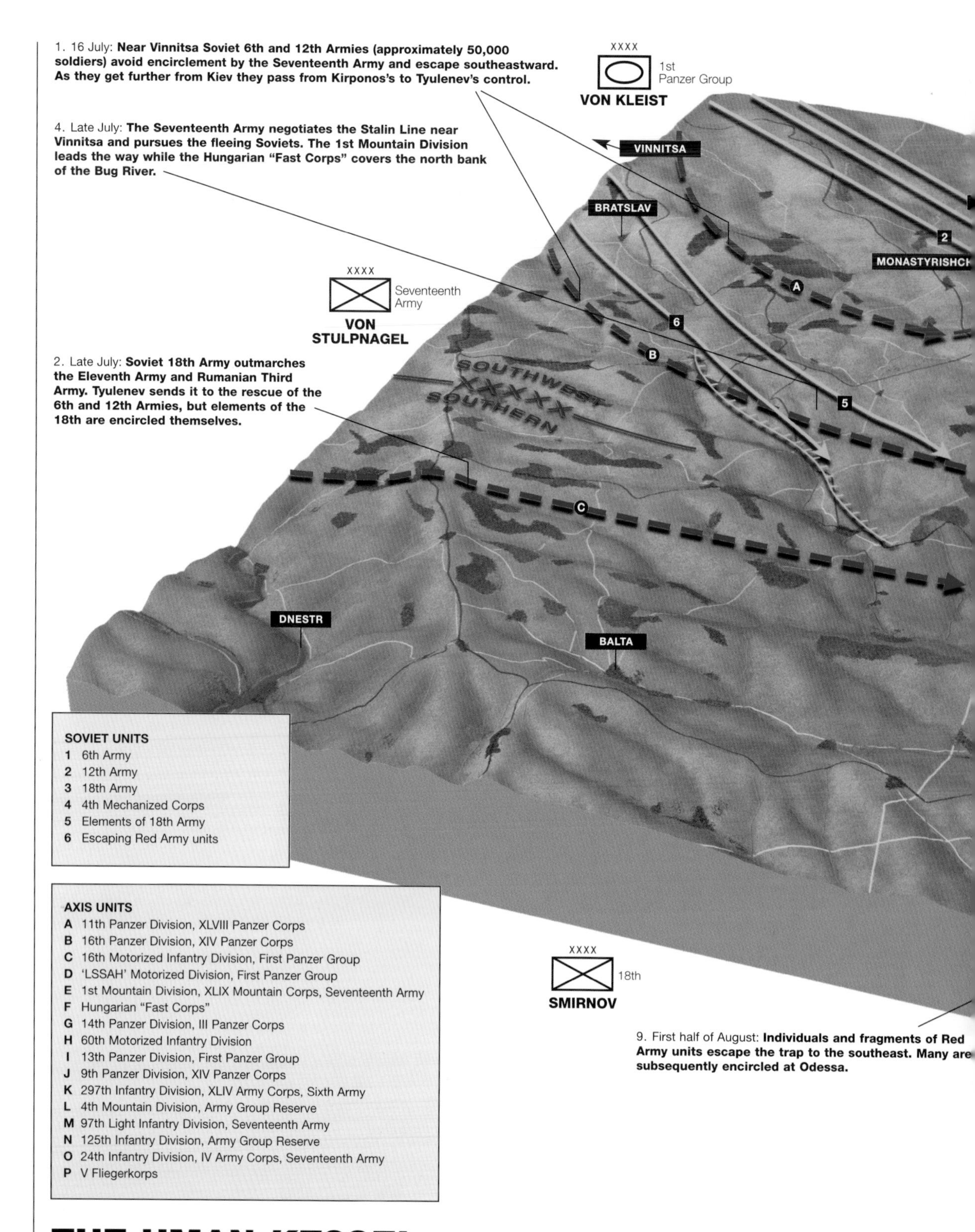

THE UMAN *KESSEL*

16 July–3 August 1941, viewed from the southeast, showing the encirclement and destruction of Muzychenko's 6th Army and Ponedelin's 12th Army by von Kleist's First Panzer Group and von Stulpnagel's Seventeenth Army.

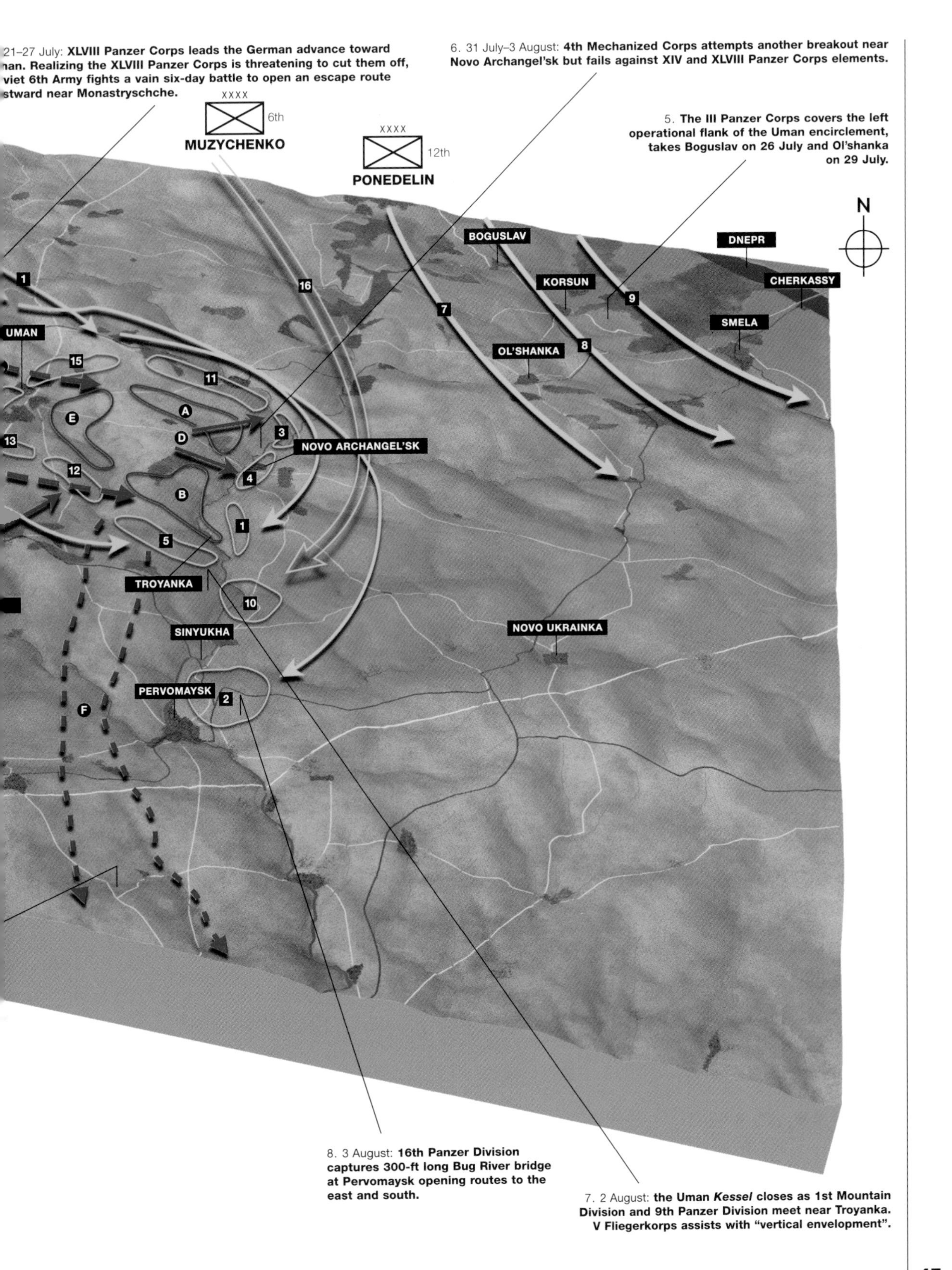

21–27 July: XLVIII Panzer Corps leads the German advance toward
nan. Realizing the XLVIII Panzer Corps is threatening to cut them off,
viet 6th Army fights a vain six-day battle to open an escape route
stward near Monastryschche.
6. 31 July–3 August: 4th Mechanized Corps attempts another breakout near Novo Archangel'sk but fails against XIV and XLVIII Panzer Corps elements.
XXXX
6th
MUZYCHENKO
XXXX
12th
PONEDELIN
5. The III Panzer Corps covers the left operational flank of the Uman encirclement, takes Boguslav on 26 July and Ol'shanka on 29 July.
N
BOGUSLAV
DNEPR
KORSUN
CHERKASSY
SMELA
OL'SHANKA
UMAN
NOVO ARCHANGEL'SK
TROYANKA
SINYUKHA
NOVO UKRAINKA
PERVOMAYSK
A
B
D
E
F
1
2
3
4
5
7
8
9
10
11
12
13
15
16
8. 3 August: 16th Panzer Division captures 300-ft long Bug River bridge at Pervomaysk opening routes to the east and south.
7. 2 August: the Uman Kessel closes as 1st Mountain Division and 9th Panzer Division meet near Troyanka. V Fliegerkorps assists with "vertical envelopment".

Uman. It created the 26th Army out of the 4th Rifle and the 5th Cavalry Corps and placed them east of the Dnepr, opposite Kanev. The 26th Army was to cross the river on 15 July and get into the rear areas of the First Panzer Group, thereby disrupting von Rundstedt's plan. However, the Germans learned of the plan when a Soviet liaison plane landed behind their lines. Alerted, Group Schwedler set a trap. The force of the Red Army's blow, launched finally on the 18th, surprised the Germans. Von Kleist faced the XIV Panzer Corps eastwards to assist Group Schwedler. This left only XLVIII Panzer heading for Uman. The Germans contained the emergency but failed to completely eliminate the threat at Kanev.

With III and XIV Panzer Corps thus diverted, XLVIII Panzer continued southward. By 21 August it reached Monastyrishche, Budenny's headquarters only 24 hours earlier. Here elements of the trapped 6th Army attacked the XLVIII Panzer's inner flank. The 11th and 16th Panzer and 16th Motorized Divisions, later augmented by the "LSSAH", stabilized the situation by the 25th. The attack collapsed two days later. The XIV Panzer rejoined the advance while the III Panzer covered the eastern flank. Meanwhile, the 1st Mountain Division led the Seventeenth Army across the upper Bug. Soviet defenders and poor weather slowed the right pincer. Losses among their horses forced the *Landsers* to leave heavy weapons behind while many marched barefoot. By the 27th von Stülpnagel broke into the open country.

Tyulenev's frustration increased. He sent the 18th Army to buttress the Uman defenses but it only became half encircled. He ordered the 4th Mechanized Corps to create an escape route. With few tanks and no surprise the attack severely tested the Germans but ultimately failed. Budenny reported to Stavka, "All efforts to withdraw the 6th and 12th Armies to the east and northeast are fruitless." The *V Fliegerkorps* contributed with a vertical envelopment. Ground units finally linked up on 3 August after the 16th Panzer Division captured the 100-yard-long Bug River bridge at Pervomaysk.

A 37mm Pak 36 and crew crushed by Soviet tanks. Although still used in large numbers during Barbarossa, 37mm guns were practically useless against Soviet tanks, especially at the long ranges common in the USSR.

Cossacks with horse artillery in the age of mechanization. Troopers wear the *Kubanka* caps and *Cherkeska* caftans. As Soviet vehicle losses continued to rise, various cavalry forces had to provide the Red Army with a mobile capability.

Tyulenev ordered Musychenko and Ponedelin to break out. The Southern Front commander complained they remained trapped "on account of a completely incomprehensible slowness." By the 5th the pocket had been reduced to an area 14 miles square. In just four days German artillery fired more ordnance than during the entire western campaign. Fighting raged inside the *Kessel* until 8 August. The Germans captured 103,000 prisoners from 25 divisions and captured or destroyed 317 tanks, 858 artillery pieces and 242 anti-tank and anti-aircraft guns.

Back near Kanev the reinforced 26th Army attacked again on 7 August. The *V Fliegerkorps* hastily redirected *Stukageschwader* 77 and *Kampfgeschwader* 51, 54 and 55 against the bridgehead. They destroyed 94 tanks in three days. Stavka decided to abandon the Dnepr on 10 August and concentrate its stay-behind forces at Odessa but much fighting continued near Kanev. By the 13th the Soviets were in full flight. Group Schwedler manned most of the broad river by 21 August. Red Army units held on for another ten days in small groups, finally evacuating the west bank on the last day of the month. The counterattack had cost little in the way of resources, but likewise failed to halt von Rundstedt's Uman operation.

Black Sea Coast

Tyulenev's defenses held opposite the Eleventh Army and Rumanian forces. But after Uman the Soviet evacuation of Bessarabia and the western Ukraine began in earnest. Von Schobert crossed the Dnester on a wide front, taking Balta in early August. Tyulenev received permission to evacuate the Trans-Dnestr and leave a garrison in Odessa. Antonescu (King Michael promoted him to Marshal on 23 August) volunteered his military to clear the Black Sea coast and capture Odessa.

Loader of 105mm artillery piece. Artillery fire exceeded that of previous Wehrmacht campaigns by a massive margin. Artillery ammunition was the largest single commodity in the German logistics system.

Von Rundstedt issued Order No.5 on 10 August, which listed three goals: destroy Soviet forces escaping from Uman; occupy the Dnepr's west bank; secure the Sixth Army north flank. Hitler directed von Kleist take the resource-rich Dnepr bend by direct route, sparing Tyulenev another encirclement. Although reinforced by Hungarians and Italians (both far to the rear and short on supply), First Panzer was too weak, too spread out and too low on supplies to mount an effective pursuit. Von Kleist's diverse objectives were Kremenchug (III Panzer Corps), Krivoi Rog (XIV Panzer) and Nikolaev (XLVIII Panzer). Nikolaev fell on 16 August. The "LSSAH" captured Kherson from Soviet Marines on 19 August while the 22nd Infantry Division secured the 700-yard-long Dnepr bridge at Berislav for the Eleventh Army.

Rumanian General Headquarters issued Order No.31 for the assault on Odessa on 8 August. The Fourth Army passed this mission primarily on to its 1st and 3rd Corps, with the 4th and 5th Corps initially supporting. Behind an impressive line of prepared defenses stood two rifle divisions and a cavalry brigade backed up by 249 guns under General G.P. Safronov. Support was also provided by 27 warships of the Black Sea Fleet. Rear Admiral Zhukov was in overall command of the garrison. Between 16 and 24 August the first defensive belt had been penetrated with heavy losses to each side. Each army counterattacked violently as advance and loss were measured in hundreds of yards. By 4 September General N. Ciuperca admitted to Anotnescu that his infantry was decimated. The Germans sent specialist battalion reinforcements but five days later Ciuperca was relieved. Axis assaults generally weakened under General I. Jacobici until coming to a halt on 22 September.

Renewed attacks began on 2 October. By 8 October Rumanian units broke into the main defensive line. Rumanian losses were often two to three times those of the Red Army. The new offensive lasted ten days. While the Rumanians planned their final attack the Soviets abandoned the port. On 29 September Admiral Oktyabrsky suggested to Stalin that the

A PzKpfw III of XIV Panzer Corps (with disinterested Soviet POWs on board) while clearing the Dnepr bend following the battle of Uman. Army Group South lost valuable time by not immediately establishing bridgeheads over this large river.

Odessa's defenders might be of more use reinforcing the defenses in the Crimea rather than merely dying in place. Surprisingly, given his "no retreat" orders, the dictator agreed. For fear of being labeled "defeatist" no evacuation plans existed. But the Soviets' careful arrangements avoided a repetition of the earlier disastrous evacuation of Tallinn on the Baltic.

The new Coastal Army commander, General I.Y. Petrov (Safronov had suffered a heart attack), decided to abandon the port early, during the night of 15/16 October. Approximately 86,000 men were shipped out previously but on that last night 35,000 men, 1,000 trucks and 400 guns left on 192 sailings. Only rearguards remained by 0200hrs. Engineers demolished port facilities and the last vessel cast off at 0510hrs. The Rumanians did not even realize the Soviets had escaped. During the siege the Rumanians suffered 96,000 casualties, almost equal to the Soviet's 102,000 and more than the 89,000 total German losses thus far in the entire eastern campaign.

Von Rundstedt's Panzers broke through the Stalin Line at Novgorod-Volynskiy on 7 July. German indecision over Kiev, however, meant the Uman *Kessel* would not be closed for nearly a month. When von Kleist did turn south operational surprise was complete. Ultimately, however, Uman represented a compromise within the German high command between those, like Hitler himself, who wanted a smaller, more certain pocket at Uman and those, like Halder, who considered a potentially larger one near Kirovograd. Von Rundstedt expertly maneuvered his meager forces against widely separated objectives, always keeping his center strong. Nevertheless, Kirponos avoided the destruction of the Southwest Front, kept Army Group South behind schedule thereby allowing Stavka to shift forces to the critical Smolensk theater.

General Muzychenko was among the 103,000 Soviets captured at Uman. Responsibility for treatment of POWs, including their murder and neglect, lay with the *Heer*, not any Nazi organization. In 1941 200,000 died in one POW camp near L'vov alone.

KIEV

Führer Directive 21 had not settled the issue of Barbarossa's main effort. One month after the invasion the German high command hit the "what next" point and required a further month to develop and execute a plan. Decision-making devolved on operational leaders; the war had little chance of destroying "the bulk of the Russian army in western Russia … in a rapid campaign" (Barbarossa March Directive, see Boog, p.593)

Genesis

Hitler never fell under the spell of Stalin's capital and by 8 July already suggested sending Guderian into the Ukraine. Halder deviously worked to dissuade the Führer, enlisting von Brauchitsch, von Bock and Jodl's behind-the-scenes help and falsifying Red Army strength estimates. Hitler issued Führer Directive 33 on 23 July and a Supplement days later confirmed the southern strategy, uniting the First and Second Panzer Groups and, to Halder's chagrin, leaving Moscow to von Bock's infantry. The Army Chief of Staff now increased estimates of Soviet forces defending Moscow hoping Hitler would decide in favor of a massive victory there. On 30 July Hitler postponed any decision on future operations until current ones – closing the Uman pocket and creating Dnepr bridgeheads – were complete.

Besides, Barbarossa had reached the anticipated logistical pause. Only two rail lines served von Rundstedt's entire army group when German doctrine called for a minimum of one per army. The *Reichbahn*'s goal of 24 trains per day in September was achieved on only 12 days, and many of those were only partially loaded. OKH ordered Army Group Center to transfer 5,000 tons of *Grosstransportraum* to its southern neighbor.

On 4 August Hitler, OKW and OKH staff met leaders of Army Group Center (including future assassination conspirator Henning von Treschkow) at von Bock's headquarters at Borisov. The generals could not discourage their Führer, however, now enthused about von Rundstedt's chances following Uman. Halder and Jodl struck a compromise; they decided not to decide on Moscow or Kiev but instead told Hitler the Wehrmacht could take both! By mid-August even Göring, as Director of Economy and Four-Year Plans and, since 29 June, Economic Director of Occupied Eastern Territories, waded into the discussion in favor of the Kiev option. Halder played his last Ace by sending Guderian to the *Wolfschanze* on 23 August. The Panzer general was in the Moscow "camp" (and not yet disgraced) but knew nothing of the compromise. He selfishly agreed with anything the Führer wanted so long as his Second Panzer Group maintained cohesion, thereby unwittingly torpedoing Halder's scheme.

These maneuverings came too late as Hitler issued Führer Directive 34 on 30 July. A Supplement on 12 August read: "the most important aim ... is not the capture of Moscow but, rather, occupation of the Crimea, the industrial and coal-mining area of the Donets Basin, the cutting of Russian supply lines from the Caucasus oil fields ..." Hitler recognized the importance of the Ukraine's resources and knew that before Army Group Center could move on Moscow, Army Group South would have to advance and cover von Bock's right flank. Accordingly OKH issued orders on 30 August for Army Groups Center and South to cooperate in the upcoming operation. Of greater significance for Germany's generals was Hitler's deepening involvement in military decisions, the abrogation of traditional Prussian prerogatives over

Soviet riflemen in action. Infantry bore the brunt of the fighting for both armies. The Red Army proved tenacious in defense, always ready to counterattack and willing to continue fighting past the point where soldiers of other armies would have surrendered.

A briefing at Army Group headquarters in Uman following the *Kessel* battle. From left at the map table are General Messe, Mussolini, Hitler, von Rundstedt and Lohr. Cap devices in the audience indicate representatives from many Nazi and Fascist organizations.

civilian authority and their inability to pull together to achieve a common goal when threatened from outside.

Similar dilemmas and problems with senior generals bedeviled Stalin. Like most Germans, many Soviets assumed Moscow to be the Wehrmacht's *Schwerpunkt.* Zhukov, however, believed Army Group Center's losses sustained fighting for Smolensk instead indicated an attack toward Kiev and told his boss as much on 29 July. Within a week Stalin replaced the marshal for again pointing out the Ukraine's vulnerability. He was wary of "fighting withdrawals" since retreating from Berdichev and Vinnitsa had resulted in the encirclement at Uman.

Three days later Kirponos confidently told Stalin that he could hold Kiev. German intelligence credited the Southwest Front with considerable forces: 73 rifle, 16 tank and five cavalry divisions (in reality respectively 30, six and two at full strength). By the second half of August the Red Air Force enjoyed a 2.2:1 superiority in fighters and a 1.5:1 advantage in bombers. Zhukov, now a front commander but still a member of the Supreme Command Staff, sent a telegram on 18 August to the same effect as his previous warnings. About this time Marshal Budenny thought he had convinced Stalin to give up the Dnepr's west bank. A few days later, however, the dictator changed his mind and decided to hold Kiev.

Stavka further complicated command arrangements by naming Budenny to lead the "Southwest Direction", supposedly coordinating the efforts of the Southwest and Southern Fronts. While German and Soviet high commands were thus occupied, in accordance with out-dated plans trains from Kharkov poured reinforcements into the trap and near certain destruction. Most often they went straight into the city rather than on the salient's flanks where they possibly could have halted von Kleist and Guderian.

G
WH
WH

WN
97 252

3RD PANZER DIVISION STORMS THE DESNA RIVER BRIDGE, NOVGOROD-SEVERSKIY, 26 AUGUST 1941 (pages 54–55)
After squandering a month of prime campaigning season, the German High Command resolved to eliminate the Kiev salient on 21 August. Army Group South would need the services of Guderian's Panzer Group, as well as von Kleists's, to execute the planned double envelopment. Accordingly, the Second Panzer Group turned away from Moscow and headed south days later. Guderian's Panzer troops easily brushed aside Bryansk Front formations Stalin had hurriedly thrown in their way. That left the Desna River as the one significant obstacle to linking up with von Rundstedt's forces in the Ukraine. The experienced 3rd Panzer Division under future Field Marshal Walther Model, drove south toward the 800-yard long road bridge at Novgorod-Severskiy. Marshal Timoshenko knew the importance of the river and its bridges and ordered a stout defense. 6th Panzer Regiment and 394th Rifle Regiment were given the mission of capturing the bridge. At 0500hrs on the morning of 26 August German artillery preparation began, while pioneers cleared a path through the man-made obstacles. The actual assault started two hours later. Model assembled a crack combat group under several reliable lieutenants who had experience seizing bridges. They faced mostly older, untrained Red Army troops. With covering fire from the regiment's tanks and concealed by dust and smoke, the Panzergrenadiers moved forward in their SdKfz 251 half-tracks, that shown here with an aerial recognition flag draped over the rear doors (1). **It also bears the tactical markings of 6th Panzer Regiment and the white "G" of Guderian's Second Panzer Group** (2). **A Gefreiter** (3) **vaults over the rear of the vehicle leading his squad into the attack. Motorcycle infantry on their Zundapp KS750s** (4) **led the way, taking heavy casualties. They eliminated the anti-tank gun at the western entrance to the bridge while Red Army troops initially resisted fiercely. Soon, however, the Soviet troops were streaming westwards to surrender to the attacking German troops, shown carrying the M1934 Karabiner 98k rifle** (5) **and the MP40 sub-machinegun** (6). **The bridge had been rigged for demolition with explosive charges in green rubber bags. Huge drums of fuel** (7) **hung from the wooden framework of the bridge and a 500lb aerial bomb** (8) **had even been placed in the middle of the roadbed. Fuse wires ran from the explosives across the bridge to the Soviet eastern bank. German pioneers** (9) **cut the wires and severed the ropes holding the fuel drums, which splashed harmlessly into the river below. Meanwhile, tanks on the west bank, such as the PzKpfw III** (10) **shown with an aerial recognition flag spread on its engine deck, fired their machine-guns at Red Army demolition teams working their way along the wooden framework under the bridge. Small arms fire hissed back and forth, but the German engineers managed to extinguish those fires the Soviets succeeded in starting on the bridge. Red Army artillery fire exploded all around the bridge, in the river and on either bank. All attempts to destroy the bridge failed, however, and at approximately 0830hrs a signal flare arched into the sky signifying it had been secured intact. Half an hour later the 3rd Panzer Division began flooding across the Desna River toward their rendezvous with von Kleist. (Howard Gerrard)**

Between the Marshes and Kiev

Kiev's prewar population exceeded 850,000. The III Panzer Corps under von Mackensen presented the first direct threat to Kiev when it rushed the city on 10 July. A surprise assault never materialized and soon Hitler redirected his valuable Panzers away from the potentially bloody fight. With Khrushchev as Commissar 160,000 civilians dug nearly 40 miles of defensive works, 20 miles of anti-tank ditches and 750 bunkers. The 1st, 2nd, 28th, 161st and 193rd Militia Brigades supplemented the 147th, 175th, 206th and 284th Rifle Divisions of Lieutenant General Kostenko's 26th Army.

The mission of taking this fortress behind the Irpen River fell to the XXIX Corps. The first assault came on 30 July but the defenders threw the attackers back. Lieutenant General von der Chevallerie of the 99th Light Infantry Division was wounded in action and soon received the Knight's Cross. The Germans regrouped and tried again to no avail.

The next onslaught began on 8 August, supported by assault guns, *Nebelwerfers* and *Stukas*. The fighting reminded World War I veterans of the worst combat in Flanders. Stretcher-bearers went forward only at night and battalion doctors worked around the clock. In one day one artillery regiment lost 26 horses to exhaustion and another drowned in a mud hole. By the 12th the XXIX Corps had not broken through. Under the 26th Army's intense artillery fire and counterattacks and to save German lives, XXIX Corps withdrew to its 7 August lines. The Soviet Union's third city could not be taken frontally.

The 5th Army's skillful defense to the north against von Reichenau was the other reason for the existence of the salient. Von Rundstedt concluded he could not accomplish his main mission – taking Kiev – until the Sixth Army front stabilized. He therefore reinforced von Reichenau with the LI and XVII Corps from OKH Reserve, the LV Corps from Army Group South Reserve and ultimately the 11th Panzer Division.

The crew of an SS 37mm Pak 36 cross a stream in their Krupp L2H 43 "Schnauzer" truck. Maintenance and supply for the bewildering number of non-standard vehicles from all over Europe multiplied the Wehrmacht's logistical woes.

At various times in mid- and late August Budenny, Kirponos and Khrushchev appealed to Stavka for permission to withdraw Potapov to shorter lines and keep pace with the retreating Bryansk Front. The high command consented on 19 August and the 5th Army crossed the Dnepr four days later. They failed to destroy the wooden bridge at Garnostoipal behind them, however. In Operation *Biber* (Beaver) the LI Corps and the 11th Panzer Division stormed the only bridge standing between Kiev and the marshes. Within 24 hours German assault parties reached the Desna River.

Kirponos ordered all Red Air Force assets against the bridge and two Il-2 Sturmoviks managed to burn the bridge with incendiary bombs. This cut off the Germans in the sand dunes between the rivers. The Soviets attacked them from all directions, while German artillery and Dnepr Flotilla monitors dueled for control of the rivers. German engineers finally repaired the bridge on 2 September, ending ten days of isolation. On the army's right the XXXIV Corps closed on Kiev from the north on 25 August. The next day the XVII Corps took Chernobyl. With its communications now secure Sixth Army units forced the Desna in numerous places. In view of the dangerous situation, on 7 September Kirponos demanded permission to retreat over the Desna. This Stalin granted two days later. On the 10th von Reichenau linked up with Second Army finally hemming in the 5th Army.

Guderian from the North

While Hitler and his top generals debated the campaign's objectives Guderian moved south with his Second Panzer Group supported by Kampfgeschwader 3 and 53, Schnellkampfgeschwader 210 and Jagdgeschwader 51. Budenny immediately alerted Stalin to the danger in the 5th Army's rear. Within a day the XXIV Panzer Corps broke Major General K.D. Golubev's 13th Army and cut the Bryansk–Gomel rail line, endangering Bryansk Front's communications. Two days later Stavka created the 40th Army under Major General K.P. Podlas, specifically to block Guderian.

In a daring action Model's 3rd Panzer Division captured the Desna River bridge at Novgorod-Severskiy on 24 August. Both sides threw forces into the fight. Stavka ordered the 21st Army to attack into von Schweppenburg's rear, but this came to naught. Red Air Force reconnaissance saw the entire situation develop but the Soviets lacked combat power on the ground. The 21st Army pulled back without telling its neighbor to the east, 40th Army. Completely unsupported, any assault into Guderian's flank by Podlas was out of the question.

To make matters worse remnants of the 13th Army disobeyed Stalin's orders and retreated away from the fight just as Model cut the Moscow–Kiev rail line at Shostka. Simultaneously the Second Army burst into action to the west of Guderian and smashed into the 21st Army, which drifted toward Kiev and eventual destruction.

Led by XXIV Panzer Corps, Guderian pushed southward. From 2 September Lieutenant General A.I. Eremenko's Bryansk Front attempted to slow them by counterattacking the exposed east flank. On 6 September Kirponos ordered the 21st Army (formally assigned to the Southwest Front that day) to drive into the rear of the 3rd and 4th Panzer Divisions – von Schweppenburg's vanguard. Eremenko's efforts failed to

THE KIEV POCKET

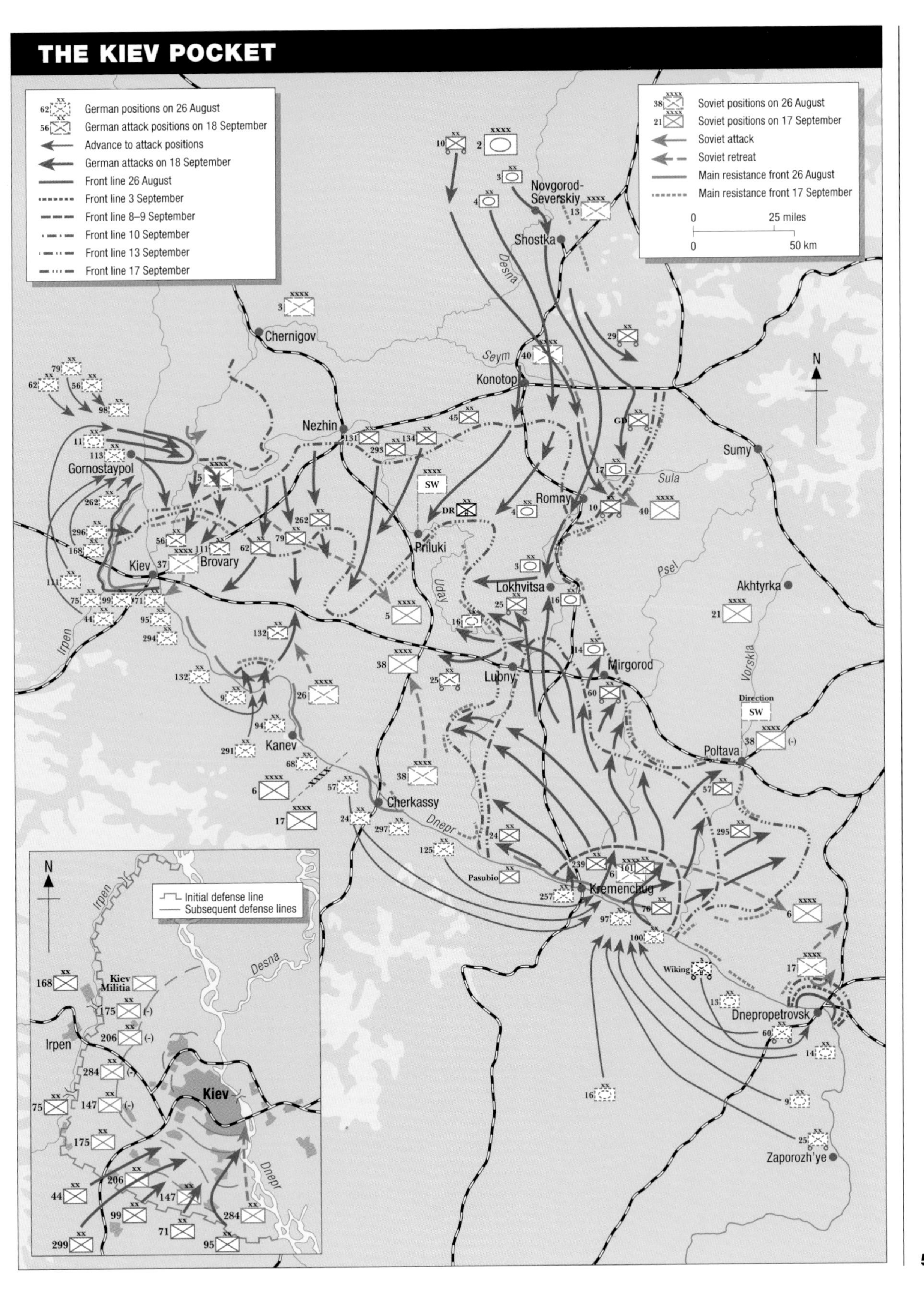

A Gefreiter holding two MP38s and another soldier stand watch over the Dnepr, the last major obstacle to Barbarossa. This photo gives a good idea of the river's width.

slow the Panzers, which crossed the Seim River the next day. A 20-mile gap now existed between the Bryansk and Southwest Fronts.

The 21st Army finally launched its assault on 9 September. Lacking coordination with the Bryansk Front it accomplished little. Later that day Stavka ordered the 5th and elements of the 37th Armies (a new headquarters controlling reinforcements arriving near Kiev) to turn away from the Sixth Army and toward Second Panzer Group. This move was also too late. The Soviets sensed a trap but could not react to the threat.

By 10 September the gap between Kirponos in Kiev and Eremenko outside grew to over 40 miles. When Model's 3rd Panzer Division occupied Romny that day Stalin ordered the Southwest Front to direct 90 percent of all its air missions against Model (including many by the new Sturmoviks). With the 40th Army ingloriously pushed aside and the 27th Army's three rifle divisions guarding 100 miles of front the Soviets' north shoulder collapsed.

The Southwest Front's line exceeded 500 miles. Budenny saw the danger represented by the First and Second Panzer Groups and requested permission to withdraw from the Dnepr to the Psel River. On 11 September he argued with Chief of General Staff Shaposhnikov over this course of action. Finally Stalin stepped in and settled the matter; he fired Budenny and instructed Kirponos to hold out. As Zhukov recommended three days earlier, the dictator named Marshal Timoshenko to command the soon-to-be-wrecked Southwest Direction.

Von Kleist from the South

Von Kleist's Panzers closed in on the wide Dnepr. The 9th Panzer Division managed to get across at Zaporozhe on 19 August but could not hold its position against determined Soviet counterattacks. Further upstream the Seventeenth Army secured a major bridgehead the next day at Kremenchug. Panzergrenadiers of the 13th Panzer Division captured a 1,000-yard bridge at Dnepropetrovsk on 25 August. The 60th Motorized Division joined in the next day and within a week the 198th Infantry Division and SS Division "Wiking" solidified the bridgehead. Intense Red Army attacks pounded the Germans from three sides but were defeated with the help of the Luftwaffe (and the first appearance of the Italian 22nd Fighter Group). At Kremenchug 80 tanks attacked the LV Corps sector in one day, of which 60 were destroyed.

In their way stood the new 38th Army. Stavka created this formation from headquarters, 8th Mechanized Corps, and five rifle and four cavalry divisions – mostly new arrivals to the front. Its 40,000 men defended a 120-mile front. The main German blow hit the 297th Rifle Division, but all Soviet reserves were to the north resisting Guderian. Dogfighting aircraft swarmed in the skies above. The 38th Army's counterattack planned for 8 September never materialized; with no armor and low ammunition it was "impossible to move in the open terrain due to aerial attacks."

While the Germans assembled for the final encirclement, Zhukov issued vain warnings. First Panzer Group left "Group Mackensen" (III Panzer Corps and the C.S.I.R.) to defend the heavily contested Dnepropetrovsk bridgehead. On 10 September von Kleist sent XLVIII Panzer Corps into Seventeenth Army's lodgment at Kremenchug. His group fielded only 331 Panzers, 53 percent of its 22 June strength. Despite heavy rains the two armies attacked on 12 September. *V Fliegerkorps* flew air

Members of the Reicharbeitsdienst (RAD) "Tomaschek" unit. Numerous paramilitary organizations competed with the military for a share of the German manpower pool. The RAD and "Organization Todt" perhaps contributed most to the military effort.

support while the II Flak Corps provided air defense and anti-tank fire for the advancing Panzers.

Hube's 16th Panzer Division led the way with 9th Panzer Division alongside pulling the corps behind them. Supported by *Nebelwerfers* ("*Stukas zu Fuss*"), the XLVIII surprised the Soviets and covered 43 miles in 12 hours. The II/2 Panzer Regiment overran the 38th Army headquarters and the commander, now Major General Feklenko, evaded capture by jumping out of a window. With von Stülpnagel covering its eastern flank First Panzer Group made for a rendezvous with Guderian.

Closing the Trap

Red Army units now had farther to go to escape eastward than the Germans did to close the trap. Sensing their pending doom, the defense stiffened on each point of the closing jaws. Model's men required two days to fight their way through Romny. On 13 September his 3rd Panzer Division raced the final 30 miles to the outskirts of Lokhvitsa, the planned link-up point with Army Group South. Simultaneously, coming up from Kremenchug, the 16th Panzer Division collided with fanatic NKVD defenders in Lubny. Hube personally led the fighting through the town. *V Fliegerkorps* contributed by isolating the pocket, keeping the skies free of Red Air Force aircraft and by preventing escape. Hube crossed the remaining 25 miles to Lokhvitsa and Guderian's men, officially sealing the *Kessel* at 1820hrs on 14 September.

That same day Marshal Shaposhnikov reminded Southwest Front "you must fulfill comrade Stalin's order of 11 September" to stand and fight. The dictator and Kirponos literally debated the issue over the tickertape as the trap closed. After Minsk, Smolensk and Uman Stalin was still ignorant of the Blitzkrieg's speed. Around Lokhvitsa the Panzer men at once turned and stood back-to-back anticipating both immediate breakout and relief attempts.

The Soviet Union's senior leadership continued its now moot debate over abandoning Kiev. Just days into his command of the Southwest Direction Timoshenko began to show signs of the strain. He sent his chief of staff, General I.Kh. Bagramian into the pocket to tempt

46TH INFANTRY DIVISION ASSAULT THE TARTAR DITCH, PEREKOP, 24 SEPTEMBER 1941 (pages 62–63)
The Eleventh Army attacked out of Rumania on 2 July as part of Operation "Munich". While its comrades besieged Kiev and executed the Uman encirclement, the Eleventh plodded across the barren southern Ukraine with no motorized formations under command. While two Panzer Armies closed the Kiev pocket the Eleventh's XXX Corps captured a bridgehead over the 750-yard wide Dnepr at Berislav. At this point the Army's beloved commander, Eugen Ritter von Schobert, died when his Fiesler Storch liaison aircraft exploded after landing in a minefield just miles east of the bridge. While an energetic new commander, Erich von Manstein, took over, reconnaissance troops of "LSSAH" Motorized Division and elements from the LIV Corps attempted to rush the Perekop Isthmus and break into the Crimea. They discovered Red Army defenses better prepared than expected and settled down for a prolonged and deliberate assault. The 46th Infantry Division fought a running battle through the town of Perekop and across the centuries-old Tartar Ditch just to the south between 24 and 27 September. Von Manstein began to shift forces toward Perekop in anticipation of the climactic battle for the Crimea. German artillery preparation began early on 24 September. Pioneers advanced through barbed-wire entanglements and other obstacles with Bangalore torpedoes, improvised demolition charges (1) **and wire cutters. They took heavy casualties despite support from German artillery, Stukas** (2) **and assault guns. Landsers advanced alongside the pioneers, providing covering fire. The squad shown here are equipped with a mixture of M1934 Karabiner 98k rifles** (3), **MP38** (4) **and MP40** (5) **sub-machineguns and MG34 light machine-guns** (6). **They are also generously supplied with the ubiquitous M1924 stick-grenade** (7). **There was no vegetation and only minimal relief to provide cover and concealment. The sun beat down as mercilessly as the Soviet defensive fire. Eventually the fire from the Sturmgeschütz III assault guns began to silence the 15th Rifle Division positions. Scaling the earthen rampart with assault ladders** (8) **the Pioneers got close enough to employ flamethrowers** (9) **and satchel charges against enemy bunkers and fighting positions** (10). **Despite admonitions by 51st Independent Army commander LtGen F.I. Kuzntsov that "Not an inch of soil be surrendered", defensive positions began to fall silent one by one. German NCOs urged their men forward across the last few yards to the crest of the earthworks. Singly and in small groups the Soviet defenders began to surrender. As the first positions fell, fighting spread left and right from the breach and medics could finally move forward to tend the wounded. No sooner had the 46th broken through the Tartar Ditch position, however, than Soviet 9th and 18th Armies of the Southern Front attacked Eleventh Army's northern flank. Von Manstein halted the southward movement of his units and instead attacked on his left. Capturing the strategic peninsula would have to wait. (Howard Gerrard)**

Kirponos to initiate a mass escape. Knowing the realities of Stalinism, Kirponos demanded "documentary" proof from Stavka. That finally arrived on 17 September at 2340hrs from Shaposhnikov: "Supreme commander (Stalin) authorizes withdrawal from Kiev." But it made no mention of actually escaping the trap nor where the Southwest Front was supposed to go.

Early the next morning Kirponos authorized his command to break out. He made the 37th Army his rearguard but Vlasov's troops never made it out of Kiev. Eventually over 15,000 men avoided the *Kessel*. Kirponos was not among them. He attempted to avoid capture with 1,000 men of his staff and the 289th Rifle Division. German soldiers ambushed the column and killed the general near Shumeikovo on 20 September.

The encirclement resembled a triangle with each side 30 miles long. Wehrmacht forces divided the battlefield into smaller pieces. The fight for the city proper began with the XXIX Corps' assault on 16 September. The 71st and 296th Infantry Divisions led the way over the same heavily defended terrain as before. They soon saw the churches and citadel of Kiev's distinctive skyline. The 95th Infantry and III/StuG Regt. 77 contributed to the reduction of numerous bunkers and dug-in tanks. On the Soviet side, loudspeakers blared Stalin's speeches in order to properly motivate the defenders.

Fighting died away by 24 September. That day explosions set off by remote control started fires that raged through Kiev for five days, killed many Germans and served as a lesson to Hitler about the dangers of combat in large cities. Rear security duty fell to "Group von Roques", consisting of three German and one Slovak security divisions plus five Hungarian brigades. The cruelty of the Nazi–Soviet War entered a new phase; with Axis troops shooting from the rim of the Babi Yar ravine the Jewish dead lay in pools of maroon below.

* * *

After three months of seemingly only pushing the Southwest Front back von Rundstedt achieved a major encirclement. The OKW War Diary gave the following account of Soviet prisoners and material losses. This does not include Red Army killed and wounded:

Army Group South	**POWs**	**Tanks**	**Artillery and Anti-Tank Guns**
Pocket (11–26 Sept)	440,074	166	1,727
Kremenchug (31 Aug–11 Sept)	41,805	279	106
Gornostaypol (4–10 Sept)	11,006	6	89
Army Group Center			
Since Gomel (20 Aug–10 Sept)	132,985	301	1,241
Pocket (11–26 Sept)	39,342	72	273
Total	**665,212**	**824**	**3,436**

The massive amounts of captured materiel allowed the Germans increased mobility, but mopping up took until 4 October. The Wehrmacht's effort was immense. Between 12 and 21 September *V Fliegerkorps* alone flew 1,422 sorties and dropped 625 tons of bombs. For a

Scorched earth: a supply dump burns on the horizon as the Red Army abandons Kiev on 20 September. The Dnepr River is in the foreground.

fleeting moment the *Ostheer* outnumbered the Red Army in the field but 1.5 million recruits joined the defenders' ranks in October and November. Stalin put Timoshenko in charge too late to change the course of the battle even if he had not imposed so many controls from above. The dictator sacrificed Kiev in order to buy time to prepare Moscow's defenses – to him a more valuable locale. Although historians will long debate the German's Kiev/Moscow decision one thing is clear: the generals may have won history's greatest encirclement battle but they lost the battle for influence in Hitler's headquarters.

THE CRIMEA

With the Sixth and Seventeenth Armies and First Panzer Group at the Kiev *Kessel* and the Rumanian Fourth Army besieging Odessa, von Rundstedt dispatched the Eleventh and Third Rumanian Armies toward the Crimea. Geologically, a massive alpine fold created the 10,000-square-mile peninsula and its 5,000ft mountains. It has a tradition of cultural uniqueness and dominates the Black Sea. Hitler wanted to eliminate this "aircraft carrier" targeted on Ploesti (thought the Soviets lacked strategic air capability) and gain a stepping stone to the Caucasus. He also wanted to woo Turkey into joining the Axis cause.

Meanwhile Tyulenev tried to re-establish a coherent defense in the wake of Uman. He had 20 rifle, one tank and several cavalry divisions to hold the Dnepr line from above Dnepropetrovsk to its mouth at Kherson. On 19 August Stavka gave him the job of containing German bridgeheads at Dnepropetrovsk, Berislav and Kherson. One week later D.I. Rybyshev replaced the wounded Tyulenev.

To Perekop

The Eleventh Army had progressed slowly for the entire campaign. It suffered isolation from the remainder of the army group, devoted much effort to keeping the Rumanians out of trouble and provided flank cover

THE CAPTURE OF THE CRIMEA

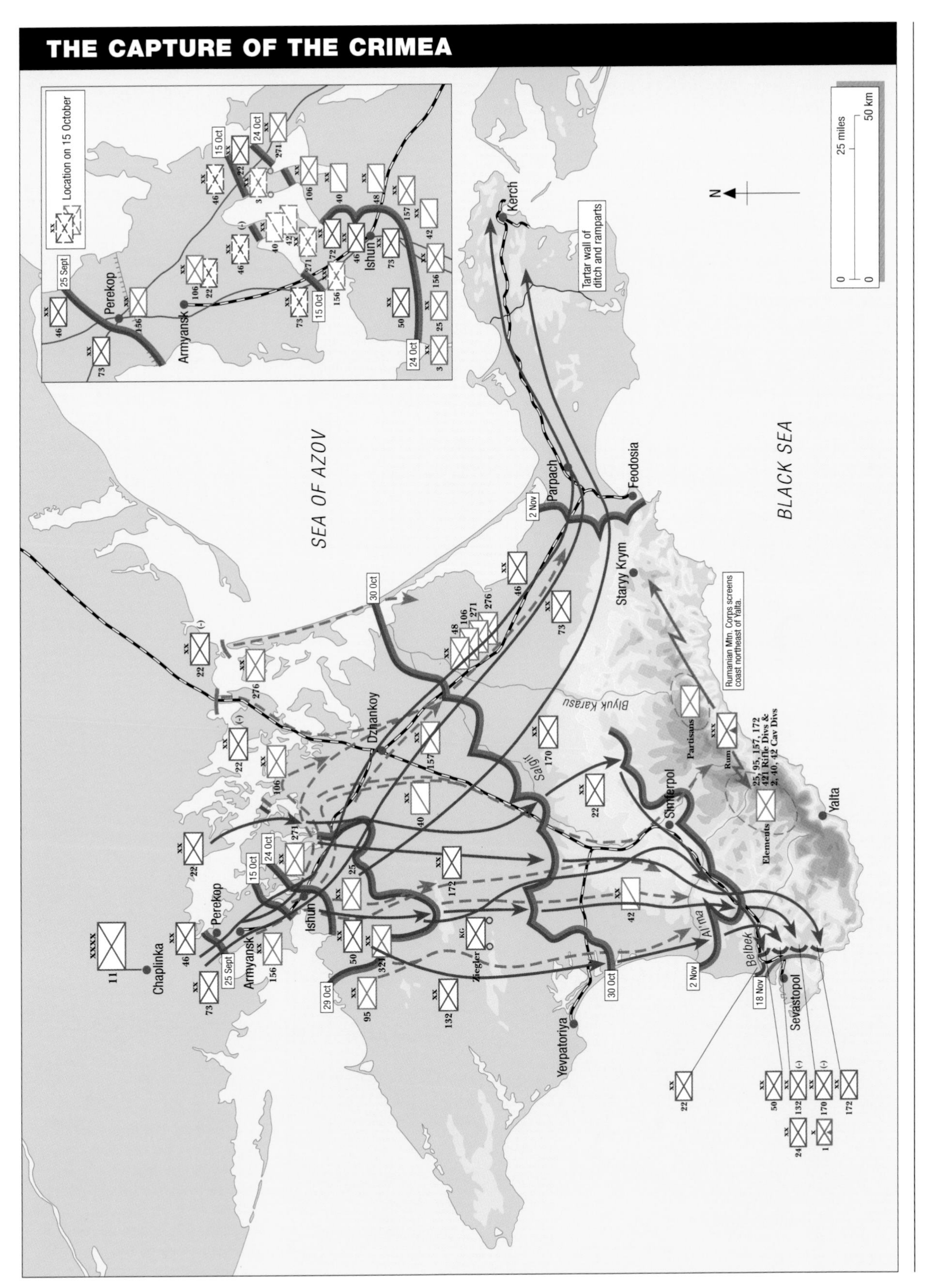

for the Seventeenth Army. Von Schobert kept his corner of Barbarossa advancing in as high morale as circumstances allowed. On 9 September von Runstedt's headquarters ordered the Eleventh Army to seize the Crimea and cover the army group's flank along the Sea of Azov. The Eleventh had begun expanding its Berislav bridgehead days before.

But von Schobert died when his Fiesler Storch liaison aircraft landed in a Soviet minefield east of Berislav on 12 September. That same day Rybyshev began pulling back to a shorter line running due south of Zaporozhe. The Reconnaissance Battalion of the "LSSAH" tried to capitalize on the confusion by dashing across the 50 miles to the Perekop Isthmus in a surprise move. It failed but in so doing discovered the Soviet defenses were much more sophisticated than expected.

Attending von Schobert's funeral at Eleventh Army headquarters in Nikolaev on 17 September was its new commander, General Erich von Manstein, newly arrived from the Leningrad Front. While he might have to work to match his predecessor's popularity he brought new energy to the Eleventh (and the Rumanian Third Army, under "operational control"). Although it took weeks to implement, one of von Manstein's first tasks was to convince his superiors the army couldn't seize the Crimea and cover the army groups' flank, and that taking the Crimea had precedence. Penetrating the defenses of the Perekop represented his most immediate concern.

The isthmus has two narrow, easily defended chokepoints, one five miles wide near the town of Perekop and another near Ishun that, while technically wider, is broken up by numerous bitter lakes. The Russians had created a massive moat 150ft wide and up to 60ft deep with an earthen bank behind it. This was known as the Tartar Ditch. Two other routes connected the peninsula with the mainland but were not militarily significant.

The Soviet 51st Independent Army commander was Lieutenant General F.I. Kuznetsov (formerly facing Army Group North). He had four rifle and two cavalry divisions in his frontline with two rifle and

Panzerbefehlswagen Ausf. E or H of 36th Panzer Regiment staff proves too heavy for wooden bridge in rural Ukraine during battle for Kiev. German engineers repaired the bridge the same day so the regiment could continue its advance.

Infantry with 37mm Pak 36 and assault gun support making the final attack on Kiev. After the losses sustained at Kiev Hitler forbade any more attacks on large Soviet cities. Losses to mechanized formations over the next year prevented Stalingrad being encircled and necessitated an assault on the city itself, with disastrous consequences.

one cavalry divisions to the rear. Defense lines were between five and seven miles deep and were augmented by bunkers, minefields and over 100 tanks. Field artillery, naval gunfire and air support were in abundance. With *Luftflotte 4* occupied at Kiev and Odessa, the Black Sea Fleet easily re-supplied the defenders. By contrast, von Manstein's railhead was way back at Pervomaysk and more to the point the Germans were considerably outnumbered.

East of the Dnepr the *Ostheer* entered the legendary steppe. According to von Manstein's plan the XLIX Mountain and XXX Corps would chase the 18th and 9th Armies toward Melitopol while the LIV Corps was ordered to Perekop. In a move that presaged Operation *Blau* in 1942, General P. Dumitrescu's Rumanians would cover the army's extended left. After LIV Corps achieved its breakthrough, the Third Army would relieve the XLIX Mountain Corps, allowing the *Gebirgsjäger* to exploit into the Crimea's interior.

Storming the narrows fell to the 46th and 73rd Infantry Divisions backed up by all the combat support von Manstein could assemble: one assault-gun and 20 artillery battalions plus *Nebelwerfers.* The *Landsers* attacked on 24 September. The watchwords were infiltrate and bypass Soviet strongpoints. Within a day Hausen's men reached the Tartar Ditch. Punished by *Stukas* and counterbattery fire, Red Army artillery slackened. The Germans negotiated the moat and wall on 26 September. In took two more days to break the first defensive belt.

Battle of the Sea of Azov

However, the last thrust would have to wait. In one of those coincidences of timing common in war, the Southern Front attacked against von Manstein's left during the last week of September. Between 10 and 13 Rifle divisions created a ten-mile gap in the Third Army's lines, through which poured two tank brigades. Von Manstein moved his headquarters away from Perekop and northeastward to reassure Dumitrescu. He also turned

3. 26 September: **Soviet 9th and 18th Armies attack Eleventh Army's north flank. Although some Rumanian units give way, the Red Army assault is too weak to threaten a major breakthrough.**

5. 28–29 September: **"LSSAH" and 1st Mountain Division halt the Soviet attack.**

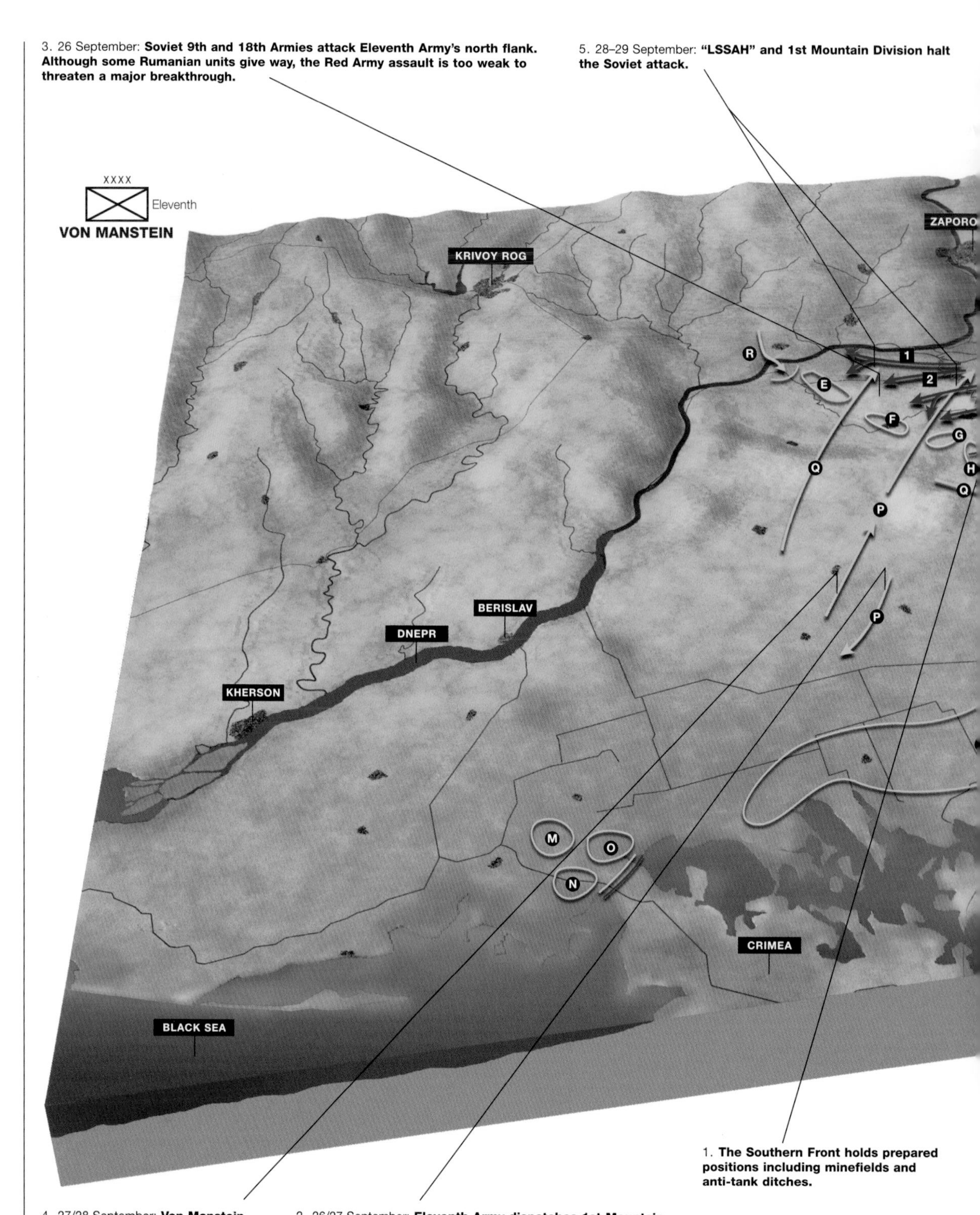

1. **The Southern Front holds prepared positions including minefields and anti-tank ditches.**

4. 27/28 September: **Von Manstein orders 1st Mountain Division to about face to prepare to attack into the Soviet flank.**

2. 26/27 September: **Eleventh Army dispatches 1st Mountain Division to Perekop to act as an exploitation force in the Crimea. Rumanian Third Army relieves XLIX Mountain Corps in a supposedly "quiet" sector.**

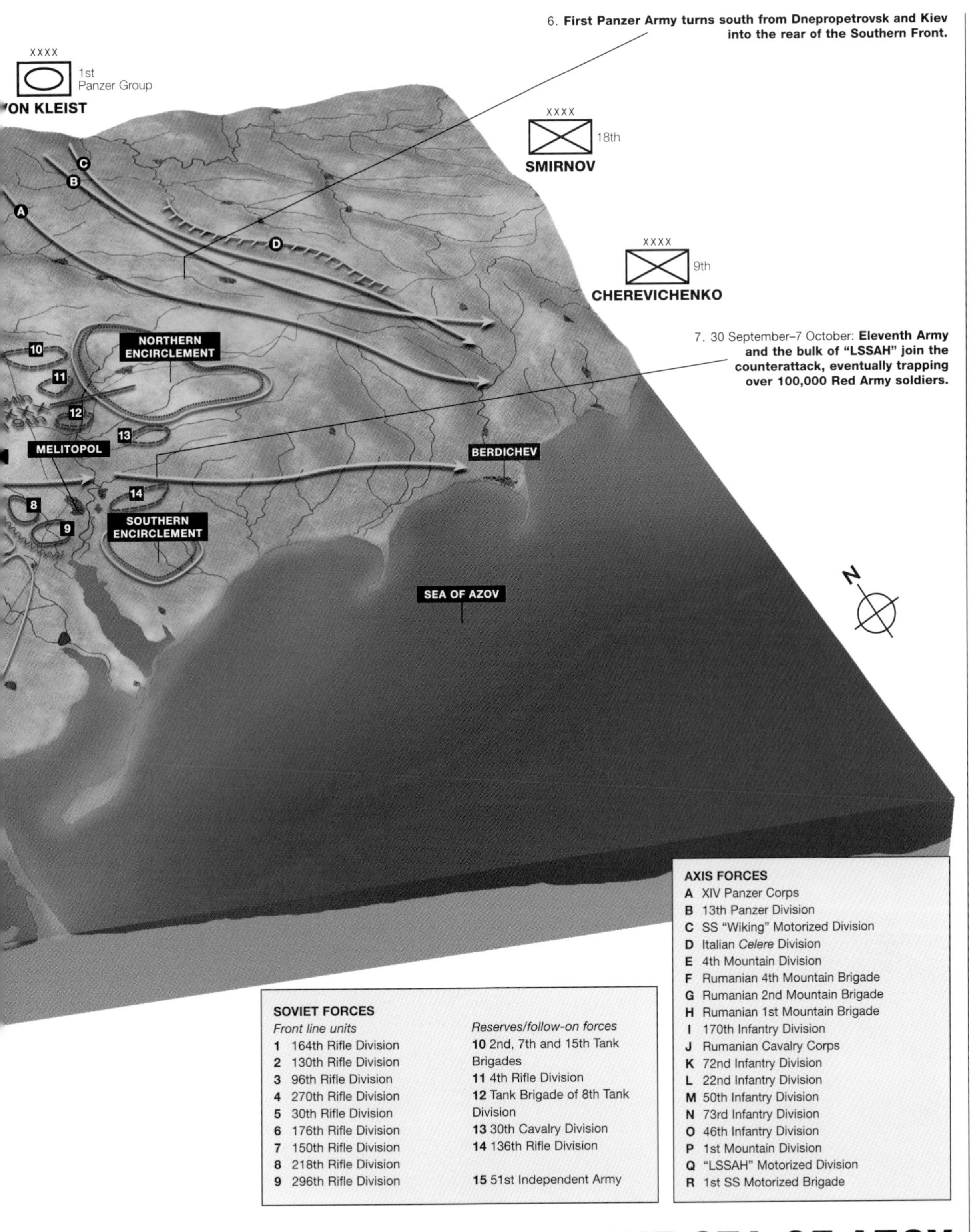

SOVIET FORCES

Front line units

1 164th Rifle Division
2 130th Rifle Division
3 96th Rifle Division
4 270th Rifle Division
5 30th Rifle Division
6 176th Rifle Division
7 150th Rifle Division
8 218th Rifle Division
9 296th Rifle Division

Reserves/follow-on forces

10 2nd, 7th and 15th Tank Brigades
11 4th Rifle Division
12 Tank Brigade of 8th Tank Division
13 30th Cavalry Division
14 136th Rifle Division

15 51st Independent Army

AXIS FORCES

A XIV Panzer Corps
B 13th Panzer Division
C SS "Wiking" Motorized Division
D Italian *Celere* Division
E 4th Mountain Division
F Rumanian 4th Mountain Brigade
G Rumanian 2nd Mountain Brigade
H Rumanian 1st Mountain Brigade
I 170th Infantry Division
J Rumanian Cavalry Corps
K 72nd Infantry Division
L 22nd Infantry Division
M 50th Infantry Division
N 73rd Infantry Division
O 46th Infantry Division
P 1st Mountain Division
Q "LSSAH" Motorized Division
R 1st SS Motorized Brigade

BATTLE OF THE SEA OF AZOV

26 September–7 October 1941, viewed from the southwest, showing the abortive offensive by the Red Army's Southern Front and the devastating German counterattack that crushes the Soviet 9th and 18th Armies and captures over 100,000 men.

MG34 crew provide the infantry anvil to the Panzer hammer on the western edge of the Kiev pocket. The three-man section includes a section leader, a Feldwebel (left), who wears the Infantry Assault badge, and a Obergrefreiter first gunner (center) and assistant gunner.

the XLIX Mountain Corps 180 degrees. Instead of punching into the Crimea it marched to bolster the shaky eastern line.

Von Manstein personally intervened on numerous occasions as the situation became tense. Rain hampered the movement of German reserves. The Soviet attack soon stalled from a combination of poor coordination, limited objectives and German resistance. Not actively involved at Kiev, von Mackensen's III Panzer Corps watched these developments from the relative quiet of the Dnepropetrovsk bridgehead. A great opportunity arose for a decisive German counterstroke. On 25 September von Rundstedt issued Order No.9 directing von Mackensen south along with the XIV Panzer Corps driving out of the C.S.I.R.'s Petrikovka salient. After crossing the Oryol and Sarmara Rivers, the Panzers' objective was Berdyansk on the Sea of Azov.

They completely outmaneuvered the Soviets. Departing on 1 October, XIV Panzer Corps on the right and III Panzer Corps swinging left cut Southwest Front's communications. Under blue skies von Kleist's men (he lost XLVIII Panzer Corps to Guderian after Kiev) put the 18th and to a lesser degree the 9th Armies in grave danger. By 3 October both were retreating and the Eleventh Army took up the chase. Two days later III Panzer Corps occupied Melitopol, the Panzer groups became Panzer armies and Y.T. Cherevichenko took over Southern Front. On 7 October, XIV Panzer Corps and the "LSSAH" joined hands and sealed the trap. The 9th and 18th Armies were crushed with a loss of over 106,000 POWs captured plus 212 tanks and 766 guns of all descriptions out of action. The Germans buried 18th Army commander Smirnov with full honors. Von Manstein redirected his attention to Perekop.

Conquest of the Crimea

Von Kleist took over responsibility for the Sea of Azov coast but von Manstein gave him XLIX Mountain Corps and the "LSSAH" as part of the deal. The Eleventh Army now had to conquer the Crimea with six infantry divisions and the promise of two more plus the small Rumanian

Rear Admiral Oktyabrsky aboard the cruiser *Krasny Krym* (Red Crimea). The Black Sea Fleet commander was also in overall charge of the defense of the Crimea and Sevastopol and led numerous joint operations.

Mountain Corps. His forces were half as strong as the 51st Army, now reinforced by the Odessa garrison (minus its heavy equipment left on the mainland). Von Rundstedt convinced Göring to provide three fighter and two *Stuka Gruppen* under Colonel Werner Mölders, the first Luftwaffe ace to both surpass the Red Baron and reach 100 victories. Mölders would land his Storch a few hundred meters behind the fighting and act as the forward air controller.

Kuznetsov had improved his positions during the battles around Melitopol. Meanwhile the flat, barren terrain offered no cover to von Manstein's men and any fighting positions they dug soon filled with salty water since the dry ground was barely above sea level. Hausen's LIV Corps again led the assault. The wider Ishun line allowed him to attack with three divisions, albeit reduced from the Perekop and Melitopol fighting. The XXX Corps would act as the exploitation force.

Artillery and *Nebelwerfers* opened up at 0540hrs on 18 October and *Stukas* joined in at sunrise. Soviet fire otherwise would have obliterated the Germans as they worked through the nine defensive lines (six miles deep) securing gaps between the saltwater lakes. After a day's progress on the east, that wing ground to a halt. Von Manstein therefore switched his main effort to his right. About this time the weather turned wet, hindering German efforts to bring supplies forward and Odessa's displaced veterans continued to reinforce the defenses. By 25 October Hausen claimed his corps was combat ineffective. Von Manstein would not hear of it, "There's no such thing for a division to be finished."

Red Army forces had suffered as well, notably from Mölders' close-air support. Kuznetsov's men finally broke on 26 October. They had no more prepared positions south of the isthmus and the retreat turned into a rout. By the 30th the front cut through the Crimea's center. Kuznetsov lost coordination between his right and left. The 51st Army made for Kerch while the Coastal Army (formerly in Odessa) headed for Sevastopol. Since von Manstein now had no motorized units, surprise moves were out of the question. Accordingly his infantry kept marching until the Soviets decided to halt and face about. By early November the XXX and LIV Corps stood in the foothills northeast of Sevastopol, which

Commander of the 1st Mountain Division, Major General Lanz, near Nikopol around the time of the Sea of Azov battle. The 1st Mountain performed masterfully on the flat steppe and consistently led the Seventeenth Army.

was defended by three divisions and the remnants of four others. At the Parpach Isthmus the newly assigned LXII Corps faced portions of five divisions. The Rumanian Mountain Corps held the partisan-filled mountains and coastline in between.

The 51st Army in the east simply could not organize effective resistance. By 3 November the XLII Corps had slipped around the defenders and captured the port of Feodosia. Denied that escape route, Kuznetsov tried to reach the larger port of Kerch at the far eastern tip of the Crimea. XLII Corps took it despite heavy fighting on the 15th, preventing further escape. In eight weeks the Eleventh Army had captured over 100,000 POWs and 797 artillery pieces of every description. But with Sevastopol unbowed to the west von Manstein would not be crossing over to the Taman Peninsula to execute Halder's grandiose expedition to the Caucasus.

Sevastopol

Similar to Singapore, during the interwar period the Soviets prepared Sevastopol for an attack from the sea. But in late 1940 and especially during the siege of Odessa they prepared for a land assault. They built three concentric defensive lines, respectively one to two, three to five, and ten miles from the harbor. Over 3,000 bunkers interspersed with nearly 140,000 mines, anti-tank ditches and trenches linked massive forts mounting naval-caliber guns. Over 100 Red Air Force planes and the Black Sea Fleet made the defense a truly joint operation.

Not only did von Manstein's infantry lack any motorized units (except *ad hoc* formations created by consolidating vehicles from existing units), but steep mountains and deep ravines surrounding Sevastopol also slowed their advance. Attacker and defender prepared for the inevitable. It was vital that Eleventh Army utilize the available logistics as effectively as possible and von Manstein used economy of force elsewhere on the peninsula in order to concentrate against the fortress. LVI Corps represented the main effort coming from the north and northeast while the XXX Corps supported from the south.

Von Manstein planned to begin his assault at the end of November but terrible weather pushed back the attack date beyond the scope of this book. Von Manstein's infantry was in a weakened state after five months of campaigning and logistics between the Dnepr and Sevastopol, 400 miles distant, were in a shambles. Eleventh Army could not attack the fortress and fight partisan bands that sprung up everywhere, especially in the Yalta Mountains. His Luftwaffe support departed to Moscow and then to the Mediterranean. The Soviets regained air superiority while the Black Sea Fleet proved capable of both resupplying the beleaguered garrison and conducting amphibious operations.

Having been denied the military honors of von Rundstedt's other armies the Eleventh finally had its chance to shine. Outnumbered on the ground it succeeded, with Luftwaffe assistance, in penetrating two well-prepared, narrow and deep defensive positions and with the help of von Kleist's Panzers it fended off an attack by two Soviet armies at Melitopol, finally clearing the entire peninsula except for Sevastopol. If von Manstein had possessed even a single mechanized division with which to race into the fortress ahead of the marching Soviets, the battle for the Crimea may have been over much sooner.

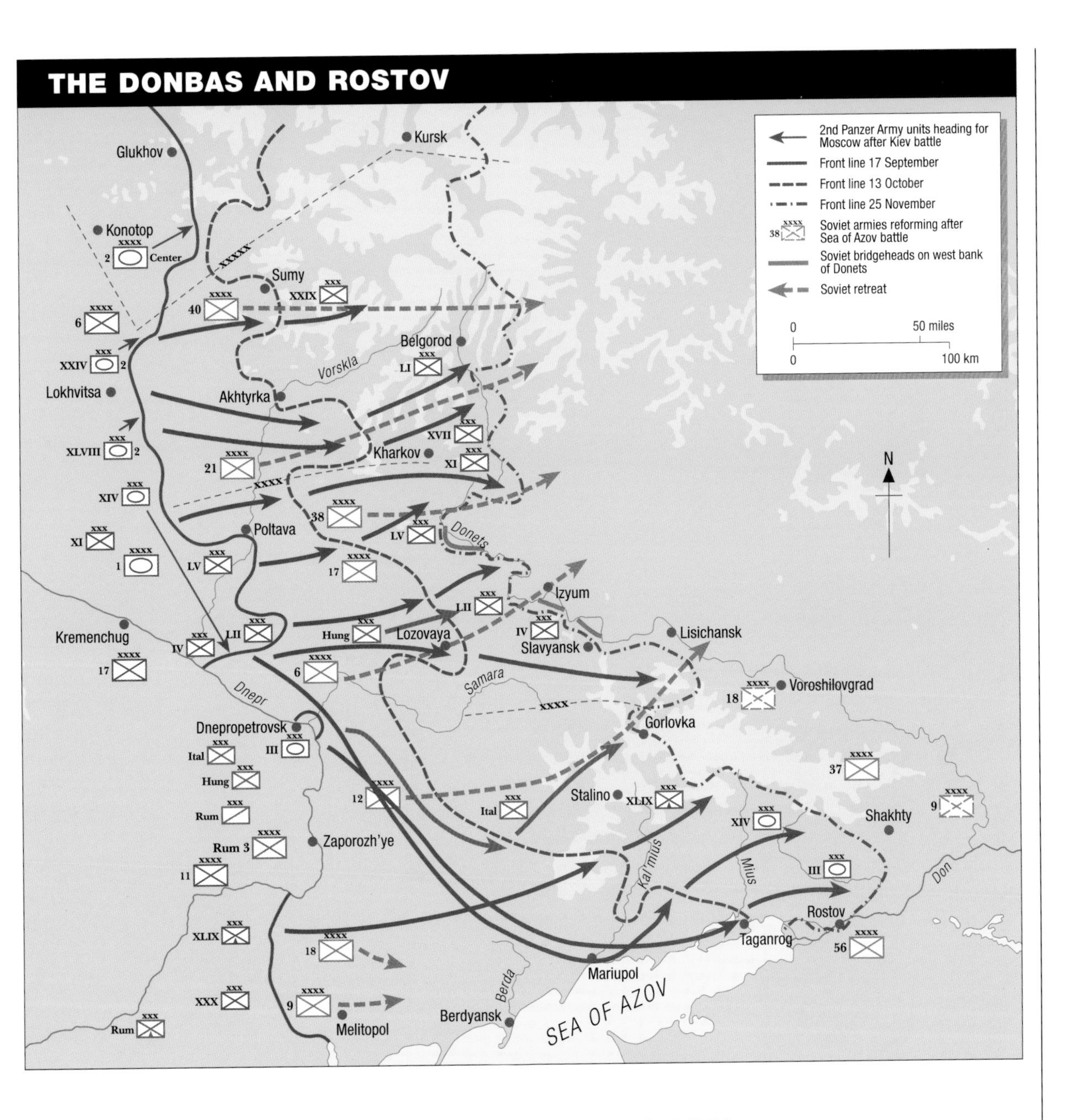

KHARKOV TO ROSTOV

Processing and sending Kiev's 660,000 POWs into captivity took weeks and delayed Sixth and Seventeenth Armies. Their next objectives were the industrial areas of Kharkov and Stalino. Believing the Soviets would continue to defend every yard of territory Hitler expected other encirclements there. First Panzer Army aimed for Rostov. The Third Reich was already short of oil and the German high command felt it had a good chance of reaching the Caucasus in 1941.

Meanwhile Stavka sought to stabilize its southern flank. The Soviet Union also depended on the steady flow of Caucasus oil and western supplies now coming through Iran. Stalin had been anxious to regain the strategic initiative since *Barbarossatag*. With much of the *Ostheer* tied

A Soviet locomotive destroyed near Tarnopol, probably by the Luftwaffe. Within weeks shortages of rolling stock and usable roadbed made themselves sorely felt. The availability of Soviet rolling stock such as this would have been invaluable at this point.

down in November facing Moscow's defenses he was keen to open offensives on either flank.

Sixth and Seventeenth Armies

Finally, on 6 October von Reichenau advanced through Achtyrka and Sumy while the Seventeenth Army moved south of Poltava. The Soviets could not organize a coherent defense. Colonel General Hermann Hoth replaced the ailing von Stülpnagel on the 10th, and pushed the Seventeenth toward Lozovaya, which fell after two days' fighting. Hoth then split his army between the twin objectives of Izyum on the left and Stalino on the right. The Sixth Army headed for Kharkov as the Soviet defenders struggled to offer more than token resistance.

Late in the second week of October wet weather and poor logistics conspired to stop the Germans. Combat had destroyed all Dnepr bridges and now ice floes threatened pontoons erected by their engineers. European-gauge railroads would not reach far enough until the end of November. Hitler stepped in on 14 October and instructed both infantry armies to cooperate against Kharkov. While this might guarantee capture of Kharkov it simultaneously weakened the German effort in the Donbas and compromised Hoth's protection of First Panzer's lengthening northern flank. The Führer lost confidence in von Reichenau, however, after the latter's uncertain leadership during Barbarossa's first months.

Stavka had no intention of allowing another massive encirclement at Kharkov and withdrew Red Army units. Improving weather in the third week of October meant increased mobility for the Germans. On 19 October Germans reported the enemy was "fighting without any enthusiasm and running away." While German Seventeenth Army battled the Soviet 38th Army southeast of Kharkov, von Reichenau curled around the north, defeating the nine Soviet divisions defending the city on the 24th. Hoth labored with his army going in three directions and the Hungarian Corps as his only mobile reserve. Soon bad weather intervened again to halt the Germans.

The Seventeenth Army crept forward. Their "pursuit detachments" consisted of infantry on native *panje* wagons. The Donbas defenders were a true Workers and Peasants' Red Army as 150,000 industrial and farm worker militia members joined regular army forces. Fighting was slow and costly in the heartland of pre-Barbarossa Soviet heavy industry. The Germans did manage to tap into the oil pipeline from Baku, acquiring many days of diesel fuel. Hoth eventually occupied most of the middle Don. The Sixth Army never made it much past Kharkov and Belgorod. For von Rundstedt's infantry the invasion ended.

Panzer Advance to Rostov

With First Panzer Army almost ineffective due to losses and lack of supply von Rundstedt recommended halting and taking up winter quarters. No one in higher headquarters supported such a move. Von Kleist's role in the battle of the Sea of Azov ideally placed his Panzer Army for continued operations toward Rostov. With von Manstein now exclusively concerned with the Crimea, First Panzer had sole responsibility for the army group's right. After Kiev von Kleist reinforced Guderian's Second Panzer Army with the XLVIII Panzer Corps and in compensation received the XLIX Mountain Corps and the "LSSAH". He arrayed his forces from north to south thus: C.S.I.R., XLIX Mountain Corps, XIV Corps, III Panzer Corps and finally the SS along the Azov coast.

Even before completing the Melitopol operation von Kleist consolidated all available fuel and pushed his right across the Mius River. Likewise, to conserve aviation gas the Luftwaffe flew only single-engine aircraft such as Bf 109s and *Stukas.* On the 20th the 1st Mountain Division captured Stalino, thoroughly ruined consistent with the Soviets' scorched earth policy. Shortly afterwards the Italians took the Rykovo-Gorlovka area. On 22 October Army Group South issued its Directive No.10 for the final assault on Rostov.

The XIV Panzer Corps' tracked elements represented von Kleist's main effort. Von Wietersheim's men crossed the Mius at Golodayevka in early November. Aided again by bad weather commencing on 7 November, the

A 20mm Flak 30 aboard an SdKfz 10/4 halftrack during Barbarossa's opening days. Even at this early stage, however, the Red Air Force was capable of making life miserable for ground troops without such accompanying anti-aircraft support.

15. 27 November: **Timoshenko renews assault along entire line. By night of 28/29 November III Panzer Corps' situation is becoming increasingly difficult. Von Mackensen abandons Rostov, with von Rundstedt's approval.**

18. 30 November: **Soviet frontline.**

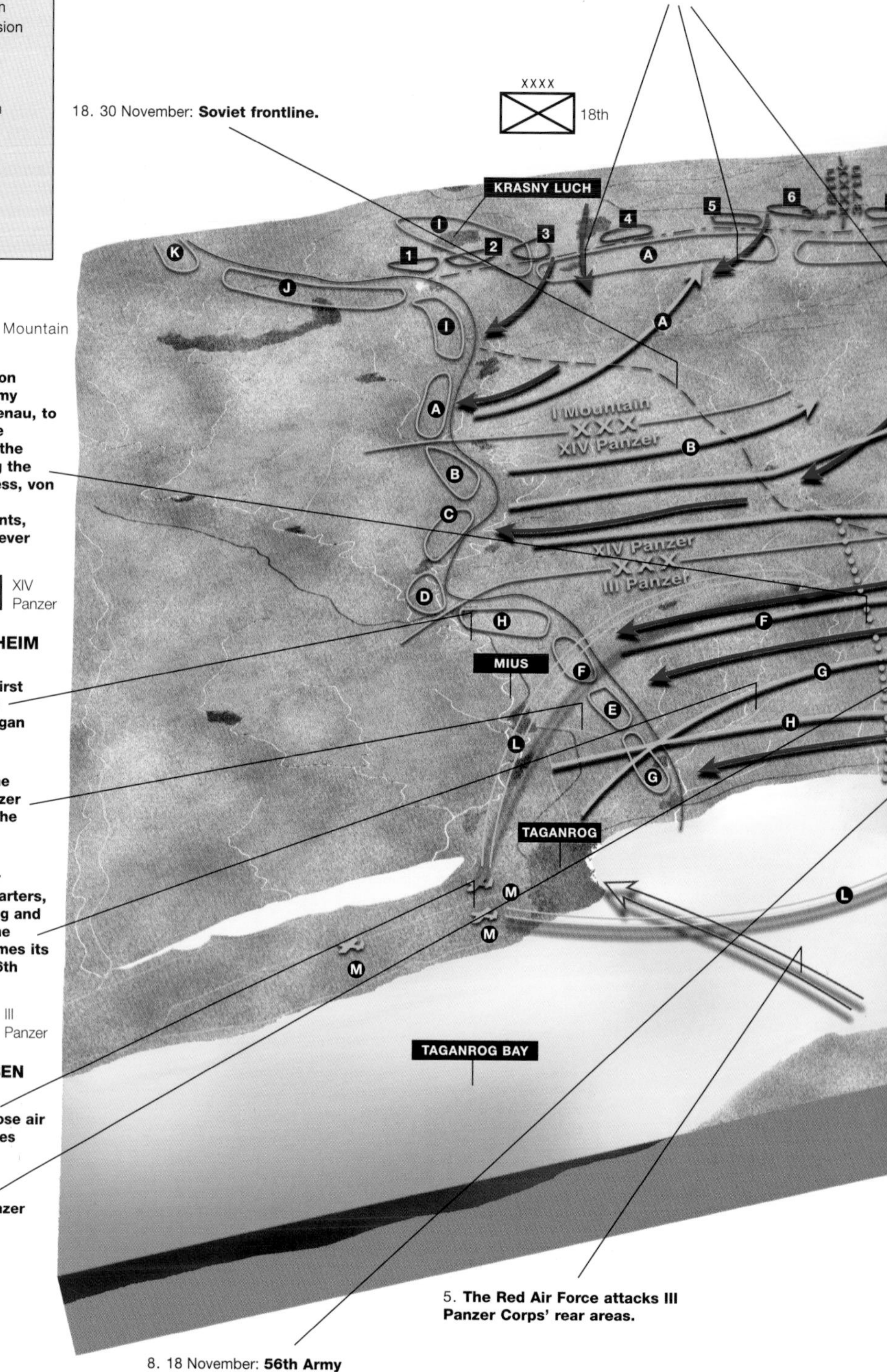

19. 1 December: **Hitler sacks von Rundstedt and orders new army group commander, von Reichenau, to halt retreat at an intermediate position between Rostov and the Mius River. After investigating the situation and finding it hopeless, von Reichenau permits continued withdrawal. Overtaken by events, the intermediate position is never occupied.**

XXX
XIV Panzer
VON WIETERSHEIM

20. 3 December: **By this date First Panzer Army reoccupies Mius position, where its attacks began 17 days earlier.**

1. Early November: **Following the Melitopol operation, First Panzer Army elements push beyond the Mius into an exposed salient.**

2. 0800hrs, 17 November: **Under pressure from Hitler's headquarters, and with its logistics improving and freezing weather hardening the ground, III Panzer Corps resumes its attack. It easily pierces the 56th Army's lines.**

XXX
III Panzer
VON MACKENSEN

4. **IV and V Fliegerkorps fly close air support against Soviet defenses and counterattacking units.**

3. 17 November: **Limit of III Panzer Corps advance.**

5. **The Red Air Force attacks III Panzer Corps' rear areas.**

8. 18 November: **56th Army counterattacks 13th Panzer Division and "LSSAH".**

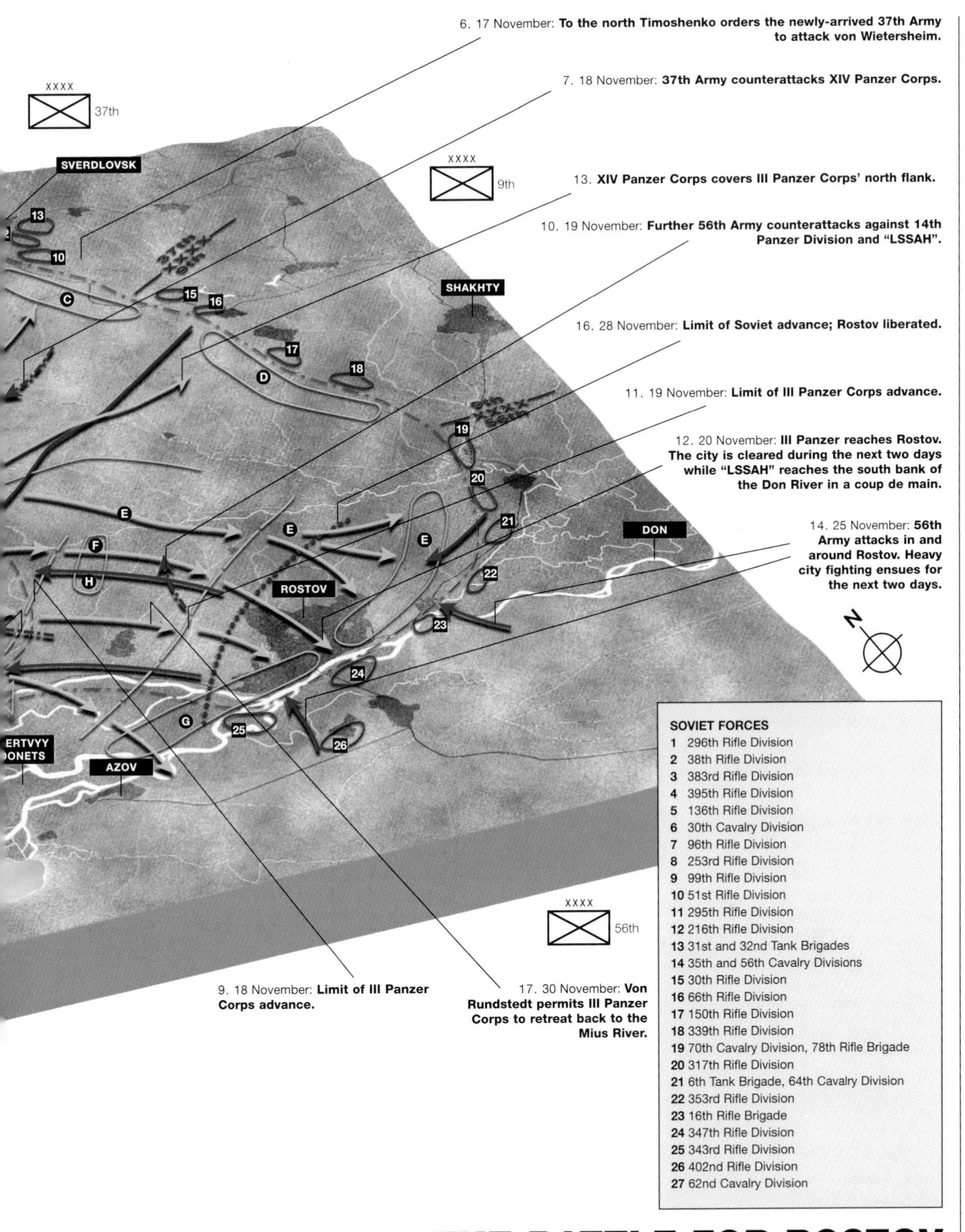

THE BATTLE FOR ROSTOV

17 November–3 December 1941, viewed from the southwest showing the see-saw battle around the strategic city of Rostov as German forces push forwards into an exposed salient and then, overstretched, are driven back to the line of the Mius River by Timoshenko's counteroffensive.

Red Army dug in south of the Tuslov River. In view of the increased resistance the main effort switched to von Mackensen. North Caucasus Front activated the 56th Independent Army under Lieutenant General F.N. Remezov to defend Rostov and the lower Don. The 37th Army commanded by A.I. Lopatin soon came alongside to extend Timoshenko's line northward.

Freezing weather returned on 13 November, permitting resumed movement. Von Rundstedt planned to continue his advance four days later, but with Seventeenth Army incapable of covering the Panzer Army's north, von Kleist's advancing spearhead soon created an exposed 150-mile flank. Timoshenko saw this opportunity and planned to counterattack.

Von Mackensen massed his armor to the north alongside von Wietersheim. Together they attacked south of the Tuslov to take an indirect route to Rostov in a clockwise sweep. Both Panzer corps moved out at 0800hrs on 17 November and quickly pierced the Soviet lines. Both air forces were extremely active: the *IV* and *V Fliegerkorps* providing close air support while the Red Air Force interdicted German supply lines between Mariupol and Taganrog.

The 37th Army's counterattack presently attracted the attention of the XIV Panzer and XLIX Mountain Corps, leaving Rostov to III Panzer Corps. By 19 November von Mackensen's Panzers reached Nachichevan, four miles northeast of Rostov, and his Panzergrenadiers occupied Aksaiskoye two miles from the Don River. The next day III Panzer Corps entered the city while the "LSSAH" even fought its way across the Don and established a small bridgehead on the south bank of the massive, frozen river. Communist Party members and civilians fled before the Panzer men. The *Ostheer*'s furthest advance was reached on 22 November with the temporary occupation of Rostov. Von Kleist wanted to abandon the city after one day but von Rundstedt ordered him to stay.

Timoshenko's Counteroffensive

On 9 November Timoshenko briefed Stalin on his plan to use the Southern Front, now under Cherevichenko, to attack von Kleist's vulnerable flank. With the bulk of the Red Army defending Moscow, Stavka could offer no additional help. The marshal assembled 12th (K.A. Korteev), 18th (V. Ya. Kolpatchy), 37th (Lopatin) and 9th (F.M. Kharitonov) Armies, in addition to Remezov's 56th Independent Army holding Rostov. Lopatin's 37th, assembling near Krasnodon, would be the main effort, with the confluence of the Tuslov and Krepkach Rivers as its initial goal. The 9th and 18th Armies, hastily rebuilt following the Sea of Azov battle, covered his east and west flanks respectively.

Timoshenko's ultimate objective was Taganrog. His force consisted of seven armies, including 40 rifle and 13 cavalry divisions plus seven tank brigades and an airborne corps. The attack's size tested contemporary Soviet command and control, but drastic measures were required to secure Caucasus oil while keeping as many Germans as possible distracted from Moscow.

Timoshenko launched his attack on 17 November and added over 100 tanks the next day. The Germans knew ahead of time but were too weak to offer much resistance along their flank. Lopatin struck portions of the Seventeenth Army, the C.S.I.R., the XLIX Mountain Corps and,

Soviet cavalry in winter clothing. The cavalry arm was well suited for operations in the winter and Marshal Timoshenko used this to good advantage during his counteroffensive at Rostov.

above all, the left flank of the XIV Panzer Corps. The boundary of these last two, held by the 1st Mountain and SS "Wiking" Divisions, was breached. The new T-34s overwhelmed von Wietersheim's Panzers and the Soviets employed *Katyushka* rockets against Army Group South for the first time. Von Kleist dispatched *Stukas* and his last reserves, the Slovakian Mobile Division (a brigade's strength).

The threat to First Panzer Army's flank and rear was real enough, but not sufficient to keep the Germans out of Rostov. Despite losing the important city, Stavka remained fixed on eliminating von Kleist. The Panzer general asked von Rundstedt for reserves and advice on stabilizing the dangerous situation. Oblivious, OKH vainly pressured Army Group South to execute Directive No.11 – a drive on Maikop in the Caucasus.

The XIV Panzer withdrew to the Tsulov River. Panzer Army headquarters pulled 13th and 14th Panzer Divisionsout of Rostov in order to create a counterattack force. Hitler's personal promise for aerial re-supply amounted to a mere 24 Ju-52s on 24 November. Von Rundstedt's staff already considered retreating to the Mius when Timoshenko lashed out again.

At 0520hrs on 25 November, men of the "LSSAH" saw battalions of Soviet infantry coming out of the fog. With arms linked and screaming "Urrah!" they stormed over the frozen Don. Without cover they fell to the German guns in their hundreds. Attack and counterattack, supported by armor of both sides, raged for two days. By 27 November the Southern Front assaulted along its entire line. Luftwaffe close air support was out of the question due to the Germans' Moscow offensive. Telephone lines hummed between Army Group's headquarters and that of Hitler. On his own initiative von Kleist ordered III Panzer Corps out of Rostov during the night of 28/29 November. Panzer divisions averaged 12 to 24 operational tanks and infantry companies numbered 50 men. Von Rundstedt approved moving to the Mius on the 30th. At 25 miles per day the retreat's pace matched that of the advance during Barbarossa's early days.

FINAL DEFENSE ALONG THE DON RIVER BY "LEIBSTANDARTE SS ADOLF HITLER", ROSTOV, 25 NOVEMBER 1941 (pages 82–83)
From their headquarters over 900 miles behind the front, Hitler, Halder and most of the Reich's leadership believed First Panzer Army should be able to push past Rostov and on to Stalingrad and the Caucasus before the weather forced a halt to Barbarossa. Never a strong German suit, Wehrmacht intelligence did not see how the Red Army could offer much of a challenge after battles like Kiev and the Sea of Azov. Somehow Army Group South scraped together enough fuel and ammunition during the first half of November to continue the advance past the Mius River. On 17 November von Kleist's men moved out. On that same day Marshal Timoshenko launched his own limited counterattack. Neither Soviet resistance, poor logistics nor harsh weather could deny III Panzer Corps, however. They entered Rostov on the 20 November and cleared the city of defenders two days later. Von Kleist had no enthusiasm for staying in Rostov and presently requested permission to evacuate. At the end of an exposed salient, weakened from five months campaigning and with its logistics unimproved, his Panzer Army was in no position to put up a serious fight. On the south edge of the city overlooking the Don River the 300 men of "Leibstandarte SS Adolf Hitler" Motorized Division's reconnaissance battalion under Sturmbannführer Kurt "Panzer" Meyer held a five-mile front. They had had only three days to improve their positions by digging into the rock hard earth and stacking blocks of ice in front of them. Early on 25 November Timoshenko loosed his 56th Army against the III Panzer Corps' defenses in and around Rostov. At 0520hrs on a dim and freezing morning, parts of three rifle and one cavalry division assaulted the German line. The mile-wide Don was frozen solid and supported all but the heaviest vehicles. T-34 tanks (1) **provided support fire from the far bank. Soviet riflemen of the 343rd Rifle Division** (2) **attacked in battalion strength with bayonets fixed to their Moisin Model 1891 rifles** (3) **standing straight up, screaming "Urrah!" and often with their arms linked. The German troops weaponry included the standard M1934 Karabiner 98k rifle** (4) **and MG34 light machine-guns** (5)**, with officers also carrying the Walther P38 sidearm** (6)**. These small arms were supported by a few Pak 38 50mm anti-tank guns** (7)**. Some of the SS troops wore issued snow smocks** (8)**, some improvised snow camouflage** (9) **while others had nothing but their standard wool uniforms** (10)**. The Soviet infantry attacked in three waves. Successive lines stumbled over piles of dead from earlier attacks, each getting closer to the defenders on the bluff above the river who fought desperately to keep control of the Don River bridge** (11)**. Finally the fourth wave broke through the 2nd and then 1st Companies of SS men. Assault guns with German infantry immediately counterattacked. They captured 400, mostly wounded, while over 300 Red Army soldiers lay dead on the battlefield. Total cost to the "Leibstandarte" Division was two dead and seven wounded. But two days later Timoshenko attacked along the entire Southern Front line and the First Panzer Army reeled back to the Mius River position. Their retreat represented the Ostheer's first operational defeat of World War II. (Howard Gerrard)**

After hours of telephone calls between Hitler's and von Rundstedt's staffs (the field marshal refused to speak directly with higher headquarters), the Führer instructed First Panzer to halt east of the Mius along an intermediate line. With *Luftflotte 4* flying overhead von Kleist's men pulled back all the way to the Mius anyway. They maintained a small bridgehead at Taganrog, mostly for its advanced airfields, but otherwise abandoned the river's east bank – a move sure to infuriate Hitler.

Von Rundstedt is relieved of command

At this juncture, with crucial battles taking place at Leningrad, Moscow and Rostov, Hitler left his headquarters for head-of-state duties in Germany. Retreat to the Mius was practically an accomplished fact when he returned from the funerals of Luftwaffe aces Ernst Udet and Werner Mölders. Von Brauchitsch, who had suffered a severe heart attack on 13 November, took the brunt of Hitler's wrath. The Führer demanded last-man defenses and counterattacks. Von Rundstedt would hear nothing of it and offered to resign, which Hitler immediately accepted.

In a teletype early on 1 December Hitler appointed von Reichenau joint Army Group and Sixth Army commander (both headquarters were in Poltava) and instructed him to halt von Kleist's withdrawal. Von Reichenau passed on the order to First Panzer headquarters and appealed to von Kleist's sense of duty. But the Panzer commander knew better the strategically disastrous implications of throwing his army back at the Soviets, and he had the wellbeing of his weary troops in mind. Von Reichenau relented late that day and confirmed the retreat order.

To personally investigate, Hitler made the unprecedented move of flying to the front on 2 December. With von Reichenau and Lohr's chief of staff he flew to Mariupol to meet von Kleist and "LSSAH" commander Sepp Dietrich. Hitler could not ignore the two frontline leaders'

Rostov, November 1941. Soviet riflemen advance through the "Gateway to the Caucasus". Rostov was the first Soviet city liberated, though the Germans recaptured it during Operation *Blau* the following summer.

The harsh Russian winter stressed further the already overstretched German logistics system. In the harshest conditions, mechanized transport often failed altogether and it was necessary to revert to more traditional methods such as the horse-drawn sleigh shown here.

unanimity. Dietrich's testimony of SS suffering and unstinted support of his *Heer* superiors impressed the Führer. Hitler left the next day, again flying via Poltava. There he met von Rundstedt, acknowledged the field marshal's service and promised to reinstate him after some rest.

This was as close as Hitler ever came to admitting a mistake to one of his generals. By late November the Army Group's hopes rested on First Panzer Army. However, gravely weakened from five months of fighting, at the end of a feeble logistical tail and poorly supported by its northern flank units von Kleist could not hope to capture Rostov and hold it for longer than a week. Across the front the Soviets began to recover from Barbarossa's initial shock, husband replacements and develop operational skills of their own. Timoshenko's counteroffensive would not be the last time the Red Army exploited an overextended German thrust. Army Group South was fortunate von Rundstedt and von Kleist were as skilled in defense as offense.

CONCLUSIONS

Of the three Army Groups, von Rundstedt's came closest to achieving its Barbarossa goals: it crossed the Dnepr, occupied most of the agrarian and industrial areas of the Ukraine, neutralized the Crimea as a threat to Rumania, captured 1,000,000 Red Army troops and killed probably as many. As with the rest of Barbarossa, however, these successes did not equal strategic victory over the USSR. Initial conquests amazed friend and foe; Göring did not believe estimates of Red Air Force planes destroyed on the ground until an actual count of captured airfields revealed claims were low.

By mid-July, however, first lieutenants commanded battalions. Unlike the campaigns in Poland and France, the Soviet Union's vastness dissipated the Blitzkrieg's shock value. By the latter stages of Barbarossa the Red Army threatened to de-mechanize the *Ostheer*. The invasion's initial plan, Führer Directive No.18, glossed over the essential element of its *Schwerpunkt*. This matter had to be settled mid-campaign. Five months later the Führer had driven the Army's commander in chief into retirement, begun to micro-manage even the smallest frontline units and handed the German generals their biggest defeat since 1806.

Battles on the frontier were brutal. Von Reichenau mismanaged the First Panzer Group (under Sixth Army control) from the time it was jammed up behind the German start-line until von Kleist received a measure of independence and freedom of action on 26 June. Kirponos wanted to counterattack but could not concentrate his mechanized corps, which was scattered 300 miles (8th Mech), 120 miles (9th and 19th Mech), 60 miles (22nd Mech) and 50 miles (15th Mech) from the front. *Luftflotte 4* insured any attacks lacked coordination. When he almost succeeded in cutting First Panzer Group off from Sixth Army, poor Soviet communication failed to inform the general only six miles separated his two pincers. With Kirponos' counteroffensive at an end both armies now raced to see which would occupy the Stalin Line first.

Stalin complained he had lost Lenin's proletarian state and went silent. German soldiers heard rumors he had escaped to China, Iran or Turkey or had been assassinated. Von Kleist's Panzers soon reached the gates of Kiev. Supporting infantry and siege artillery was nowhere to be seen. So far Kirponos had avoided destruction and kept Army Group South behind schedule. This permitted Stavka to reinforce the Western Front fighting on the Moscow axis.

While the Soviets expected von Rundstedt to turn north against their capital at any time (many German generals wanted the same thing), he pivoted his Panzers southward to Uman instead. Kirponos had few tanks after the frontier battles to halt such a maneuver. He launched a flank attack over the Dnepr at Kanev. Von Greim dispatched one *Stuka* and three bomber squadrons to the area until the *Landsers* stabilized the

The less glorious side of war. Germans pause to bury their dead in a ceremony repeated often by both sides. The advancing Germans could at least honor their fallen comrades, the retreating Soviets usually could not.

situation. In place of a modest *Kessel* at Vinnitsa the Seventeenth Army and First Panzer scored a major victory at Uman – the Army Group's first major encirclement. The victory was tarnished, however, when von Kleist lost time clearing the Dnepr bend instead of racing for bridgeheads over the massive river. As Paulus later wrote, securing these crossings "proved to be very prolonged and costly."

On the far south flank the Eleventh Army and two Rumanian armies moved out along the Black Sea coast. Some German units had walked all the way from Greece. Soldiers of the Rumanian Mountain Corps marched "barefoot for two or three weeks." By mid-August, however, they achieved von Rundstedt's first operational objective by encircling Odessa. Left to the Rumanians and supported by the Black Sea Fleet, the port proved a tough nut to crack. The Eleventh Army continued on to the land bridge to the Crimea, but the 51st Independent Army halted them just in time.

Von Reichenau, on the Army Group's extreme left, continued to struggle. His Sixth Army had won no big victories, was stuck near the Rokitno Marshes against the pesky 5th Army and watched the Seventeenth Army and Kleist's First Panzer Group grab all the glory. Its one bright spot was Operation *Biber*, the Dnepr crossing at Garnostoipal. Afterwards, Sixth Army initiated a half-hearted pursuit through the Kiev pocket and Kharkov. Hitler blamed the Army Group situation on "that egoist von Reichenau" and Halder likewise never forgave him.

Despite Halder's behind-the-scenes machinations in favor of attempting to take Moscow, Hitler remained true to his, and Barbarossa's, goal of destroying the Red Army in the field and looking forward to satisfying Germany's material needs via Ukrainian resources. After squandering a month of prime campaigning weather on re-affirming the *Ostheer*'s purpose, making logistical arrangements and quashing Halder's near mutiny, the Germans spent the month of September executing the tremendous *Kessel* east of Kiev. Hitler's generals could not present a unified front; Jodl considered turning the Second Panzer Group south the "perfect solution" to getting von Rundstedt on schedule.

On 5 August Zhukov lost his job pointing out Kiev's vulnerability. Later that month Soviet aerial reconnaissance saw Guderian's Panzers coming south but only the weak 40th Army barred his way. Stavka smelled a trap by early September but could not make a decision on how to proceed. Despite a month's delay at German headquarters, the *Ostheer* still operated well within Stavka's decision-making cycle.

The battle had four phases: 1. Securing bridgeheads over the Dnepr and Desna Rivers, 21 August–9 September. 2. Pushing toward Lockvitsa, 4–16 September. 3. Fighting for Kiev proper, 13–19 September. 4. Clearing out the pocket, 14–27 September. Some Soviet armies migrated to their destruction inside the trap while Stavka ordered others to die in place. The pocked compared to Belgium in size.

The issue of the Kiev encirclement battle is one of the most contentious of Operation Barbarossa, and indeed of World War II. Many see the potential capture of Moscow as the Brobdingnagian checkmate of the Stalinist state and likewise the decision to devote Army Group South and a large portion of Army Group Center to the encirclement at Kiev as the worst example of Hitler's desire for the quick reward in an ultimately futile operational-level conquest. Two facts support the German's actual course of action: the threat to von Bock's right and von Rundstedt's northern flanks posed by unvanquished forces ignored at Kiev and the resilience and will to survive of the USSR. Soviet plans to continue fighting past a potential loss of Moscow are well documented. The real issue is a month wasted on indecision and bureaucratic infighting within the German leadership.

After an interruption caused by the Soviet offensive at Melitopol the Eleventh Army set to work against the Crimea. The narrow Perekop Isthmus challenged von Manstein. With the support of more than six bomber, five fighter, three *Stuka* and two close air support *Gruppen*, the Eleventh broke into the Crimea's interior after an eight-day struggle. Soviet resistance plus poor weather combined with the lack of surviving bridges over the Dnepr, no siege artillery, little ammunition and other support requirements to slow von Manstein's advance on Sevastopol. Unable to take the city, von Manstein had to wait seven months to conquer the Crimea.

Army Group South suffered serious dispersion of effort following Kiev. It gave von Bock's drive on Moscow nine divisions, including two Panzer and two motorized. *Luftflotte 4* could not concentrate but supported the Crimean operation and the pursuit to the Don, fought the Black Sea Fleet and interdicted Soviet railroads and rear areas. The Army Group's logistics were not functioning adequately. It expected 724 trains to reach its bases on the Dnepr in October but received only 195. The Italians' closest railhead remained 600 miles to the rear in Hungary. Von Rundstedt's troops in the field starved while five trains per day shipped food from the "Ukrainian breadbasket" back to the Reich.

Von Rundstedt wanted to go into winter quarters, establish a firm defense and prepare for further operations in 1942. Halder would not hear of it and Hitler ordered Army Group South to make one last lunge to gain Don and Donets River bridgeheads for the next year. Soviet recuperative powers continued to amaze the Germans. On 21 October the OKH vainly ordered the Sixth Army to Voroshilovgrad, the Seventeenth Army to Stalingrad and the First Panzer Army to Maikop! Even refueled with oil captured in the Baku-Stalino pipeline, von Kleist barely made it to Rostov.

Following the debacle on his southern front at Kiev, however, Stalin installed a new commander: Marshal Timoshenko. He fortified the

A Ukrainian woman laments destruction of her village. Civilians paid a brutal toll during the fighting all around them.

resurrected Soviet defenses and looked for any opportunity to sting the Germans. He singled out the Panzer spearhead at Rostov and chased von Kleist back to the Mius River. Within a week the momentum switched to the Red Army, Hitler cashiered von Rundstedt and Barbarossa ended for the southern wing. Days later Germans streamed back along most of the front.

Within strategic and political constraints first Kirponos and Tyulenev and later Timoshenko worked wonders in the Ukraine. Unexpected numbers of Mechanized Corps and motorized Anti-tank Brigades including 120, 76 and 85mm guns plus thousands of mines surprised the invaders. So did modern Soviet tanks, such as the KV-1, which in one case took over 100 37mm hits at under 300 yards range with only minor damage to its turret traverse mechanism. Poor intelligence and wishful thinking meant the Soviets' ability to recreate lost forces caught the Germans unprepared.

Nevertheless, von Rundstedt's men also performed masterfully. His Army Group alone conquered an area greater than that of France. It is appropriate to quote the bulk of his Order of the Day (15 August) following the battle of Uman: ... *I am proud to stand at the head of an Army Group whose troops execute all their tasks with the highest devotion and combat readiness and meet the enemy daily in fierce combat ... I repeatedly express my thanks and unreserved appreciation for all those outstanding efforts ... However, the campaign has not been won. We must keep pressure on the enemy and allow him no quarter, for he has many more reserves than we ... I request all command authorities find the means to create short recuperation breaks for their exhausted formations, during which they can be removed from the front and, for one day get the rest they need. During these recuperation breaks don't harass the troops with training. They should get their fill of sleep, dedicate time for personal hygiene and mending their clothes and equipment, and if possible, further refresh themselves with increased rations.* Personnel losses were horrendous. One-fifth of German casualties were killed in action while 5 percent went missing in action. The remaining three-quarters were wounded or POWs who

STRATEGIC OVERVIEW

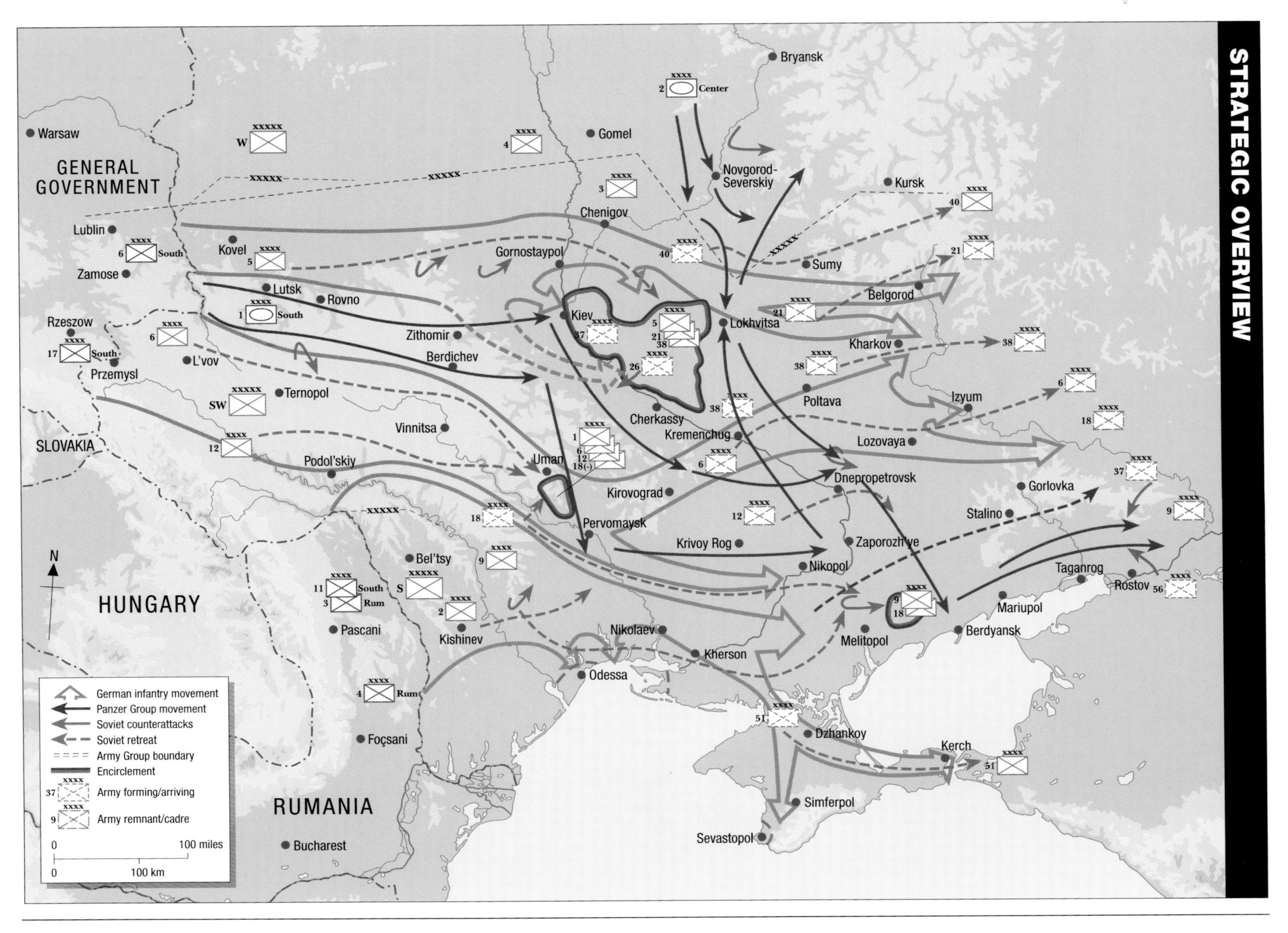

eventually returned to duty. The figures given below detail the damage caused to the Southwest and Southern Fronts by the III Panzer Corps and von Mackensen's own losses:

Theater, Dates	CUMULATIVE SOVIET Soviet POWs	Tanks Dest/Capt	Guns Dest/Capt	CUMULATIVE GERMAN KIA (Off)	MIA (Off)	WIA (Off)
Frontier, 22 June–10 July	14,500	868	472	806 (65)	388 (3)	2426 (124)
Kiev, 11–22 July	16,800	932	622	1294 (95)	448 (4)	3846 (194)
Uman Flank, 23 July–12 Aug	28,900	940	759	1642 (120)	500 (6)	5095 (233)
To Dnepropetrovsk, 13–25 Aug	62,100	1281	1350	2015 (135)	508 (6)	6442 (279)
Dnepropetrovsk Bridgehead, 26 Aug–29 Sept	96,300	1304	1509	3215 (178)	625 (7)	11,097 (439)
Melitopol–Mius, 30 Sept–5 Nov	118,400	1423	1856	3805 (204)	667 (8)	13,517 (548)
Rostov, 6 Nov–2 Dec	137.9	1506	2116	4214 (223)	814 (10)	15,356 (638)

One can see the Germans' heaviest losses came during two periods: the initial 18 days breaking through fresh Soviet units and holding off Kirponos' counterattacks, and while defending their own bridgehead at Dnepropetrovsk. When advancing their casualties were noticeably lighter.

The Southwest and Southern Front leadership suffered no catastrophic breakdown as occurred elsewhere along the battle lines. Army and corps commanders were generally capable given their lack of combat experience, poor communications, Luftwaffe interdiction and uniformly unfavorable situation. Major disaster occurred when they were caught by a surprise German move (Uman), their actions were dictated by Stavka (Kiev) or they were ordered to execute desperate measures (Sea of Azov battle). Strategically the Soviets held the best cards, small comfort to Red Army generals and soldiers in the field.

Operationally and tactically von Rundstedt was in the strongest position. This won him engagements and battles but not the war. The field marshal himself was caught between a rock (Hitler above him) and a hard place (too few, under-motorized forces in a huge country bitterly defended). But he performed well and is guilty of few mistakes. Von Kleist and von Stülpnagel performed flawlessly and presented Army Group South with most of its victories (Uman, Kiev and Don/Donets). Von Schobert labored under the twin handicaps of weak allies and more Soviet forces than he could deal with. Von Manstein arrived late but is often considered to be amongst Hitler's very best anyway. Von Reichenau's leadership can only be described as mediocre. He never employed his Sixth Army as intended but instead was out-generalled by the 5th Army under Potapov and needed constant relief from either OKH reserves, Army Group headquarters, First Panzer Group or even von Bock's Army Group Center. Ultimately, for all that wore the *Feldgrau* the prospect of Barbarossa was much brighter than the reality.

THE BATTLEFIELD TODAY

The bulk of the fighting described in this book took place in the recently independent country of the Ukraine. While under Soviet domination Ukrainian cultural identity was squashed. The Soviets deported Ukrainians, imported Russians and suppressed the language. The country suffered environmental disasters such as that at Chernobyl nuclear power plant in 1986. Since gaining independence in 1991 the Ukrainians have been building their new country – Europe's second largest. With some difficulty they are incrementally moving toward representative democracy and a market economy.

Despite an understandable pride in their heritage and nationhood, World War II (they also use the term "Great Patriotic War") remains a central part of the Ukrainian experience. This is especially true of the World War II generation, those who thrived under the Soviet system and those who have not done well since 1991. For example, while statues of Lenin and Stalin have disappeared from many public places, those of Lenin especially simply moved to locales frequented by World War II veterans and older, nostalgic Ukrainians.

The Ukraine suffered differing amounts of damage during the war. Over 80 percent of the capital and cultural center, Kiev, was destroyed. Much damage occurred during fighting in 1941 and 1943. However, retreating Red Army units caused massive destruction during Barbarossa as part of Stalin's "scorched earth" policy. Unfortunately, when the Soviets rebuilt Kiev they did so in an ugly, poorly constructed socialist style. On the other hand, L'vov (Called L'viv in Ukrainian) escaped much fighting in 1941 or 1944 and is still a beautiful example of a large eastern European city. Small villages and dirt roads characterize the countryside today much as they did during Barbarossa.

Every settlement has a small monument commemorating the war and often listing its war dead. Solitary tanks on pedestals are often the centerpiece. Signs identifying battlefields or sites of major fighting are not common. Driving in the Ukrainian countryside is recommended for the stout-of-heart only. Trains are an inexpensive and efficient way to see the Ukraine. Dirty but ubiquitous buses are a good way to visit obscure locales while rubbing elbows with the natives.

Some significant Barbarossa sites have disappeared, notably along the Dnepr River. Huge dams above the river's mouth, at Dnepropetrovsk and upriver from Kiev have created reservoirs that inundated such bridgeheads and battlefields as Berislav, Cherkassy and Gornostoipal. One also looks in vain for many scenes of fighting, such as Stalino, now called Donets'k. The Ukraine has one major museum devoted to World War II in Kiev, along with its huge "Motherland" monument to civilian and military casualties. Smaller museums can be found in L'vov, Kharkov and Odessa.

BIBLIOGRAPHY

Bergstrom, Christer, and Mikhailov, Andrey, *Black Cross, Red Star*, Pacifica Military History, 2000.
Blakemore, Porter, *Manstein in the Crimea*, PhD. Dissertation, University of Georgia, 1978.
Boog, Horst, ed., *Germany and the Second World War*, Vol. IV, "Attack on the Soviet Union", Clarendon Press, 1998.
Carell, Paul, *Hitler Moves East*, Ballantine, 1971.
Clark, Alan, *Barbarossa*, William Morrow, 1965.
Van Creveld, Martin, *Supplying War*, Cambridge University, 1977.
Davis, C.R., *Von Kleist*, Lancer Militaria, 1979.
DiNardo, R.L., "The Dysfunctional Coalition", *Journal of Military History*, Oct. 1996.
Dunn, Walter, *Hitler's Nemesis*, Greenwood, 1994.
Ellis, John, *Brute Force*, Viking, 1990.
Erickson, John, *Road to Stalingrad*, Westview Press, 1984.
Erickson, John, and Dilks, David, eds., *Barbarossa*, Edinburgh University Press, 1994.
Fugate, Bryan, *Operation Barbarossa*, Presidio Press, 1984.
Glantz, David, *Barbarossa*, Tempus, 2001.
Glantz, David, and House, Jonathan, *When Titans Clashed*, University of Kansas, 1995.
Glantz, David, ed., *The Initial Period of the War on the East Front, 22 June–August 1941*, Frank Cass, 1993.
Goerlitz, Walter, *Paulus and Stalingrad*, Greenwood, 1974.
Gorodetsky, Gabriel, *Grand Delusion*, Yale University, 1999.
Haupt, Werner, *Kiev*, Podzun, 1964.
Haupt, Werner, *Army Group South*, Schiffer Military History, 1998.
Jacobsen, Otto, *Erich Marcks*, Musterschmidt, 1971.
Jentz, Thomas, ed., *Panzertruppen*, Schiffer Military History,1996.
Koral, V.E., et al, "Tragic 1941 and Ukraine", *Journal of Slavic Military Studies*, March 1998.
Lanz, Hubert, *Gebirgsjaeger*, Podzun, 1954.
Lewis, S.J., *Forgotten Legions*, Praeger, 1985.
Loeser, Jochen, *Bittere Pflicht*, Biblio Verlag, 1988.
Von Lüttichau, Charles, unpublished manuscript, Ft. McNair, Washington, DC.
Von Mackensen, Eberhard, *Vom Bug zum Kaukasus*, Vowinkel, 1967.
Magenheimer, Heinz, *Hitler's War*, Arms & Armour, 1998.
Von Manstein, Erich, *Lost Victories*, Presidio, 1984.
Von Manstein, Ruediger, *Manstein*, Bernard & Graefe, 1981.
Megargee, Geoffrey, *Inside Hitler's High Command*, University of Kansas, 2000.
Messe, Giovanni, *Der Krieg im Osten*, Thomas Verlag, 1948.
Mierzejewski, Alfred, *The Most Valuable Asset of the Reich*, University of North Carolina, 2000.
Mitcham, Samuel, *Men of the Luftwaffe*, Presidio, 1988.
Moynahan, Brian, *Claws of the Bear*, Houghton-Mifflin, 1989.
Muller, Richard, *German Air War in Russia*, Nautical and Aviation Publishers of America, 1992.
Muller-Hillebrand, Burkhart, *Germany and its Allies*, University Publishers of America, 1980.
Nafziger, George, *German Order of Battle, Infantry in World War Two*, Stackpole Books, 1999.
Niehorster, Leo, *The Royal Hungarian Army, 1920-1945*, Axis Europa, 1999.
Schueler, Klaus, *Logistik im Russlandfeldzug*, Peter Lang, 1987.
Seaton, Albert, *Battle for Moscow*, Stein & Day, 1971.
Sharp, Charles, *Soviet Order of Battle in World War Two*, Nafziger, 1996.
Spahr, William, *Stalin's Lieutenants*, Presidio, 1997.
Statiev, Alexander, "The Ugly Duckling of the Armored Forces", *Journal of Slavic Military Studies*, June 1999.
Sterrett, James, Southwest Front Operations, June–September 1941, MA Dissertation, University of Calgary, 1994.
Tarleton, Robert, "What Really Happened to the Stalin Line?" parts 1&2, *Journal of Slavic Military Studies,* June 1992 and March 1993.
Topitsch, Ernst, *Stalin's War*, St, Martin's, 1985.
Weinberg, Gergard, *World at Arms*, Cambridge University, 1994.
Willmott, H.P., *The Great Crusade*, Free Press, 1989.
Winters, Harold, *Battling the Elements*, Johns Hopkins University, 1998.
Zaloga, Stephen, and Ness, Leland, *Red Army Handbook, 1939–45*, Sutton Publishing, 1998.
Zhukov, Georgi, "The War Begins: The Battle of Moscow" in *Main Front*, Brassey's, 1987.
Ziemke, Earl, and Bauer, Magda, *Moscow to Stalingrad*, Military Heritage Press, 1988.

INDEX

Figures in **bold** refer to illustrations